WILL MY RABBIT GO TO HEAVEN?

'Who made God?'
'Do all worn-out grannies go to heaven?'
'Where is the deep end in the sea?'
'Why doesn't the sky fall?'
'Why do we fight?'
'Where did I come from?'
'Why won't you have Daddy back?'
'How do we catch electricity?'

Have you ever been floored by a real poser of a question from a four-year-old? Or by a genuine enquiry about some delicate topic from a thoughtful nine-year-old? Children's natural and healthy curiosity about the world around them, and the people and situations they encounter, can lead to some mind-boggling questions.

In this book Jeremie Hughes, minister's wife, journalist and mother of two, has brought together answers to a wide range of questions children ask – about death and suffering, about God, about sex, about heaven and hell.

'It won't give you all the answers. But it may just help you out of the embarrassing moment when junior pops a question in the supermarket queue or at Sunday tea with Granny. It may also answer some of the questions *you've* always wanted to ask . . .'
Parentcare

'Some of these questions and children's comments . . . are hilarious but the topics covered are serious and of concern to many parents and teachers of young children.'
Contact teachers' magazine

D0012568

TO NIC AND HELEN

Will my rabbit go to heaven?

AND OTHER QUESTIONS CHILDREN ASK

Jeremie Hughes

A LION PAPERBACK
Tring • Batavia • Sydney

Published by
Lion Publishing plc
Icknield Way, Tring, Herts, England
ISBN 0 7459 1221 4
Lion Publishing Corporation
1705 Hubbard Avenue, Batavia, Illinois 60510
ISBN 0 7459 1221 4
Albatross Books Pty Ltd
PO Box 320, Sutherland, NSW 2232, Australia
ISBN 0 86760 945 1

First edition, under the title *Questions Children Ask*, 1981
Reprinted 1981, 1983, 1984, 1985
This new revised and illustrated edition 1988

British Library Cataloguing in Publication Data
Hughes, Jeremie
    Will my rabbit go to heaven?: and other
    questions children ask.—New, rev. and
    illustrated ed.
    1. Children's questions and answers
    2. Christian education of children
    I. Title   II. Hughes, Jeremie. Questions
    children ask
    200   BV4529
    ISBN 0-7459-1221-4

Library of Congress Cataloging in Publication Data
Hughes, Jeremie
    Will my rabbit go to heaven?
    (A Lion paperback)
    1. Children—Religious life.   2. Children and
    philosophy.   I. Title.
    BL625.5.H84   1988   230   87-29310
    ISBN 0-7459-1221-4

Extracts at the beginning of each chapter are reproduced by
kind permission of the following copyright-holders: 'Explained'
from *Now We Are Six*, by A. A. Milne, Methuen Children's
Books/Dutton; *Watership Down*, by Richard Adams,
Rex Collins/Macmillan; *The Last Battle*, by C. S. Lewis,
Collins/Macmillan; 'I wonder' from *Come Follow Me*, by
Jeannie Kirby, Evans Brothers; *The Railway Children*, by
E. Nesbit, J. M. Dent/Puffin.
The Hiding Place by Corrie ten Boom is published by
Hodder and Stoughton/Fleming H. Revell Company.

Printed and bound in Great Britain
by Cox and Wyman, Reading

Contents

Author's acknowledgments

I would like to express my gratitude to the many people who contributed to this book, especially: to the children whose inquiring minds provided the questions and in some cases, the answers; to Wendy Green who filled in many gaps due to my inexperience of 'city life' and who also wrote the poem 'Three into one will go'; to Rosemary Bancroft whose inspired talk led to this book; to Ann Davey; to the two medical friends who helped me with answering the questions on sex; to the many teachers who provided further questions and answers including biologist Pat Heath, Mary Morris, Liz Hawkins, Anne Purdon, Janet Mackenzie; to parents, and in particular the two mothers who bravely shared their children's bereavement experiences; to Jean Howitt; to Philip Marsden; to a group of Margate mums; to Joan, who gave up her spare room to me and a typewriter. Last, but definitely not least, my special thanks to my own personal theology adviser, my husband Chris, for his help, patience and encouragement.

For help in updating and additions for the new edition, my special thanks to Caroline Philps, the teachers and children of St Paul's C of E Primary School, Tipton; teachers Sylvia and Karen; the Rev. Ian Lewis and members of the congregation at Holy Trinity Church, Platt; Grace Wyatt of the Charnwood Centre for handicapped and normal children; the Rev. Richard and Dr Joy Moore; Wendy Titman of Kidscape; Vivienne Aitchenson, St Giles C of E First School, Ashtead – and many others.

Introduction

It's always in a crowded bus, when that elderly neighbour has come to tea, or when we are elbow-deep in the household chores, that the most mind-boggling questions arise.

Children choose their moments, don't they? And, sometimes, those very questions are just the ones that we as adults dare not ask and to which we'd dearly love to have the answers.

Even three- and four-year-olds are bursting with questions about anything and everything – from 'How is frost made?' to 'When will I die?' Sometimes we need to stop and look deeper than the actual question to see what they are *really* asking.

We are supposed to live in a society where no subject is considered taboo. To talk about sex is the norm. But are we equally prepared to talk about death? And the subject of God is ignored, or at best politely tolerated.

Children nowadays come up with questions that their parents or teachers would not have dreamed of asking until a much later stage in their development. Television and education make children much more aware than we were of what is going on around them and in the wider world. Primary school playground chat includes words and phrases that previous generations would not have heard of until well into their teens. Even seven-year-olds are asking about Aids, rape, homosexuality, death and suffering, as well as familiar old chestnuts like 'Who made God?' and 'Does Granny need her specs in heaven?'

Children expect answers to their questions and usually

want them instantly! It's all too tempting to reply 'Oh, not now dear, we'll talk about it later. Can't you see I'm busy?' Or, if we're asked a question on sex, 'You'll have to ask your mum/dad' or 'You're too young to understand that now'. But 'when you are older' may be too late. They probably won't ask us then.

We can't possibly know *all* the answers to children's questions. And sometimes the moment they choose really *is* inconvenient. But there is no need to fob them off. It's better to say, 'We'll sit down later and look it up in a book', or 'We'll ask so-and-so when we see them next'. And make sure we don't forget. Occasionally, it may be right to say 'I'll explain it later', as long as it's *not* because we can't be bothered to think about it. We also need to beware of telling a lie or even a half-truth to get out of a sticky situation – we're bound to get caught out later on!

To many questions there can be no stereotyped answer. The age, understanding and experience of the child must all be taken into consideration. Young children asking questions about God or sex usually want a quick, simple answer (not that the answer *is* always simple, especially to some of their 'God' questions!). They don't want a theological or physiological lecture.

It's easy to forget the language barrier that exists between child and adult. When we know the answer, have the experience and the knowledge, it's still difficult to communicate exactly what we mean in simple enough terms to make sense to the child. How, for example, do we answer a four-year-old's 'What is electricity?' And what would you expect a child to understand by the phrase 'Wait and see what's round the corner'?

'Don't give your child mental indigestion,' warned a teacher-friend who has two lively boys of her own. 'It's important to answer only what they have asked and not to overload them with information. At the same time, don't underestimate their levels of understanding. Much depends on the age of the child. And, sometimes, when we've thought they understood our replies and taken in the information, the same old question crops up later on and they appear to have forgotten everything we previously told them. It's helpful to make all the answers as relevant as possible to the child's own experience of life. And it's equally important to allow children to see that we do not understand everything ourselves.'

Wise advice! 'But Mummy, I thought you knew everything!' said a shocked eleven-year-old.

We need to listen with our hearts as well as our ears, for sometimes the question asked is not the problem that's really on their minds. This means taking time to communicate with children, giving them individual attention, and patience if it's something serious and difficult for them to talk about.

As far as possible, with younger children, all adults involved in a situation should give consistent answers to the questions raised. At some point, of course, our children will receive from other people answers which differ from our own and they will have to seek the truth and find out for themselves. With older children, it's good to let them know that ours is not the only viewpoint on some issues.

Not all children ask their questions direct. But that's no let-out for parents! Sometimes we need to feed in information to stimulate the questions. It's by asking that children gain information to build on previous knowledge – and to go on asking more.

This book really began as a discussion between eight mums with children of primary school age, helped by one mum whose four children have now left home. We'd met to share some of the questions our children had been asking, in particular questions about God and death. Out of that came a newspaper article, and the book has grown from there.

Those who, like myself, are Christians, do not claim to be able to give their children all the answers to their questions concerning life, death and relationships. But we do believe in God as the source of knowledge, who created us to be 'whole people', spiritually, emotionally, mentally and physically. We believe he wants us to use the minds he has given us to discover the deep truths of life, to follow his plan for our own individual lives and to live peacefully in his world. He shows us the way he wants us to live – through his Spirit, through the Bible, and through our fellow Christians. And this book is written in the belief that the Bible is relevant to twentieth-century situations and problems.

Questions on how and why things work go beyond the scope of the book and are therefore not included. There are many good books on the subjects children ask about, including encyclopaedias, dictionaries and the Bible itself. However, there are spiritual dimensions to many questions that relate to life and relationships. And Christianity is all about life and relationships.

The questions have been collected from a wide range of children aged between two and eleven years old, living in town and country areas.

The answers suggested can only be guide-lines. Some, I am only too aware, are incomplete. (None give the full answers an adult would require – see the booklist.) Scientific and 'technical' questions have been treated at a level that children can understand. Others could include alternatives, and a few questions have not been answered at all. Most of the answers have come from teachers, parents and those who have experience of the relevant situations. Our ability to answer children's questions depends very much on the answers we ourselves have found to the questions of life – both great and small.

1

Questions about God

Elizabeth Ann said to her Nan:
'Please will you tell me how God began?
Somebody must have made Him. So
Who could it be, 'cos I want to know?'
And Nurse said, 'Well!'
And Ann said, 'Well?
I know you know, and I wish you'd tell.'
And Nurse took pins from her mouth, and said,
'Now then, darling, it's time for bed.'

From *Now we are Six*, by A. A. Milne

Does God really like bishops when they dress up?

I don't want to go to church today – I don't want to meet the ghost.

Doesn't it get rather noisy for God when we all pray at once?

'What does the vicar wear under his dress? Knickers or pants?' Big six-year-old brother: 'Trousers of course!'

Is God a ghost or an Irishman?

'I wonder if God loves people who are bad and steal from shops?' Reply from a six-year-old: 'God loves people who are bad but not what they have done wrong.'

Why can't we see the stable now?

Because it's fallen down. Dad says so.

Where did chickenpox come from? I suppose God had it and passed it on.

God doesn't weigh much, does he?

Doesn't he? Why not?

Because you said he was light.

When they ask questions about God, children can be very practical. Their questions can arise in the most unexpected places and often demand immediate answers. So, if you just happen to be gazing into someone's trolley in the supermarket check-out queue and your child pipes up with, 'Who made God, Mum?' you will have to think fast! At the very least, your answer will alleviate the boredom of others waiting alongside you!

Who made God?
(question from a three-year-old)
No one. God was there before the world was made. He made us and everything in the world. He was there at the very beginning. If someone had made God, he wouldn't be God.

How old is God?
(three-year-old)
God doesn't have an age. He doesn't grow old like we do. And he never changes. (To an older child we could explain that God is not restricted by time in the way our world is.)

Before there was an earth and the rest of the universe, where did God live?
(an eight-year-old)
No one knows the answer to that question – because God is not like us. He doesn't live in just one place at a time. He is everywhere. Our minds can only understand a certain amount. They would go 'pop' if we could be shown the whole universe, let alone see back in time. But one day God will let us know the answers to all the questions that have puzzled us. Doesn't Dad ever say, 'I'll have to explain that one later'? Well, one day God will do just that.

Children are naturally curious about what God is like. These are some of the questions asked by five- to eight-year-olds.

Is God human like us?
Is God made the same as us?
Is God black or white?
Does God ever go to sleep and wake up again?
Does God ever wear clothes?

God is not the same as us. He doesn't have a body. If he had, he could only be in one place at a time instead of being able to look after everyone in the world at once.

So he doesn't have a skin – black or white. And he doesn't need clothes to keep his body warm.

God's never asleep. If he went to sleep there'd be times when we couldn't talk to him.

But when God made the first people, he made them like himself in other ways. We're not like him to look at. But we can love one another, as God loves us. We can make things. And we have minds so that we can think.

God sent his Son, Jesus, into the world to help us understand what he is like. We know by reading about Jesus that God loves and cares for us, and that he wants what is best for us. He is always ready to help.

My Mum says God is everywhere and can see everything. But how can he?
(seven-year-old)

Because he isn't like us. We don't really know or understand how. But the Bible tells us he is everywhere, not just in one place, and that he can see us all, and knows everything that's going on. Jesus said that God can see even a little sparrow that falls on the ground.

It's because he can be everywhere and see everything that he can take care of everyone in the world.

*   *   *

Who made the first man and lady?
(five-year-old)

God did. The Bible tells us that he made men and women to

be company for each other and to look after the animals, birds and plants. He also made them so that they could become his special friends.

If scientists say that we come from apes, why does the Bible say that the first people were Adam and Eve?
(ten-year-old)
Science is answering different questions from the Bible. The Bible tells us who made the world (God) and why. Scientists are trying to find out *how* it all happened. The idea that people gradually developed from ape-like creatures is still only a theory. We cannot absolutely prove it. But even if we could, it doesn't mean that the Adam and Eve story is untrue. The Bible doesn't spell out *how* God made us. What it does tell us is that we are made to his design. There is a difference between people and animals. Unlike the rest of the animal kingdom, we are able to respond to God and become his friends.

God also gave us freedom to choose how to behave. The Adam and Eve story tells us how men and women at the very beginning chose to please themselves and take no notice of what God said. And that choice led to the presence of evil and pain and death in the good world God had made.

Why does the Bible say God made the world in six days? My encyclopaedia says everything evolved over thousands of years.
(seven-year-old)
The Bible 'day' does not necessarily mean our day of twenty-four hours. It could be a way of describing a very long period of time. The Bible tells us what God did, and the special place people have in his creation. It doesn't set out to give us a timetable of events.

Why did God make all the other planets?
(seven-year-old)
God had a 'master-plan' for the universe when he created it.

We can still see and understand only a little of it. Our own planet is only a very small part of the universe, and so are the other planets in our solar system.

Just by looking at our world, we know that there is a reason for everything God has made, and that nothing is wasted. We don't yet know the reason for the planets. It's possible that life on earth depends on them in some way – just as we depend on the warmth of the sun.

Why did God make everybody different? It would have been easier for him to use the same pattern.
(practical eight-year-old)

In a way he did use the same general pattern. But he made some of us males and some of us females, to help one another and to continue the human race. He made each of us a bit different, because each one of us is unique and special to God. Being different makes life more interesting – and we can tell one another apart! (Every one of us has a unique fingerprint pattern.)

As well as being different to look at, we each have different gifts – things we're good at, and things we're not. So we all need one another and can learn to work together. By making us different, God has taught us to depend on one another.

If God can see into the future, why did he make Adam and Eve when he knew they'd choose wrong?

When a mum and dad make a baby, they know that he or she will grow up into a child who can choose right or wrong. They trust and hope that with love and a good home their child will learn to make the right choices. That's what being human is all about. If we didn't have freedom to choose, we'd just be robots. God wanted us, of our own free-will, to choose to enjoy his love and friendship. That's why he made us. But there's always the risk that people will turn away from him. Think what we'd have missed if God hadn't taken the risk! We wouldn't be alive to ask why. Considering the way we have disobeyed him and made the wrong choices, it's amazing that God goes on loving us and is so patient with us.

I can't understand about Adam and Eve and them eating the apple. What's that got to do with good or bad?

(eight-year-old)

Every day, all of us are faced with choices: where to go, what to say, how to behave. Sometimes we choose what is good, sometimes what is bad. Sometimes we are happy together, sharing and laughing; at other times we squabble and make God, ourselves and everybody around us unhappy. It was just the same for Adam and Eve. There was only one thing God said that Adam and Eve must not do: they shouldn't eat the fruit of one particular tree in the Garden of Eden (it doesn't actually say 'an apple'). But they thought they knew better. They disobeyed God, and that was bad. Afterwards they were very unhappy. And ever since that time people have tended to choose to do wrong things rather than right.

If God created the world, Adam and Eve, why didn't he put Satan on his own planet and allow him to have his own people?

(ten-year-old)

We don't really know the answer to that. But we do know that God wanted people to be free to choose between good and evil. And we know that God allows Satan to test us partly to see if we really love God and want to please him. But Satan can't do just what he likes. God sets the limits, because he is in control.

What does God do all day?

(four-year-old)

What does Daddy do all day? What does Mummy do all day? We work to look after one family. God loves and looks after his people everywhere, so he has lots to do – taking care of them,

Why did God make stinging nettles?

listening to them, and answering their prayers. At night when we are asleep people on the other side of the world are awake, so he is still busy then.

Why is God playing hide-and-seek with me? I can't find him?

(four-year-old)

We can't see God, but he's not teasing or playing hide-and-seek. The Bible tells us he is with us always, even though we can't see him as we can other people.

Why didn't God help me find my toy when I asked him?

(disappointed six-year-old)

Why didn't God mend my bicycle when I asked him?

God isn't a magician. He uses people to do much of his work. Daddy will mend the bike when he gets home/Mummy will help you look for your toy. God does help us when we ask him. He may help you remember where you put that toy. But he doesn't always put things right just when we want. We have to learn to take care of things.

Why did God do so many miracles in the Old Testament times like when Daniel was in the lions' den, but he doesn't do them today?

(eleven-year-old)

God does miracles today too, but we don't always hear about them, and sometimes we don't recognize them. Many times he heals people. It's a miracle each time someone turns to follow God's way instead of his own. A criminal can change from crime and violence to loving and helping others.

We know about the miracles in the Bible because they're written down. But the Bible covers a very long period of time and only a small area of the world. Most of the Bible miracles came at certain special times.

I've never seen a miracle like Daniel being saved from the

lions, but I have read of amazing happenings in different parts of the world and here too – people being cured of drug addiction and of serious illness.

What colour is God?

God doesn't have a body or skin like ours. But Jesus had brown skin when he was on earth, like all the other people in the part of the world where he was born.

What does 'Amen' mean?

It means 'may it be so', 'may it happen'. It shows that the prayer is finished – a kind of 'over and out' to God. If we say it after someone else's prayer it means we agree with what they have said: we're all praying the prayer, not just the person who actually said it.

What does 'eternal' mean?

Eternal means something that has always existed and will always exist. It's outside time, so it never ends. God is eternal. He is the same, 'for ever'. And he gives his own eternal, 'for ever' life to all those who become Christians and follow Jesus. We can have that special new life here and now, while we are on earth. And it continues when we go to be with God when we die.

*   *   *

It does not take a child long to realize that although Jesus is talked to, sung to and read about, he cannot be seen physically. In the middle of a Christmas Day service, a bright two-year-old asked, 'Why isn't Jesus here today on his birthday?' On another occasion, a three-year-old wanted to know why Jesus was never in at church. Knowing that Thursday was the day the local vicar came in to take assembly, a five-year-old asked, 'Is Jesus coming to school today?'

Many children come up with a variety of questions on this theme: 'How do you know Jesus is here?', 'Why can't I feel him?', 'If Jesus is everywhere, why don't I bump into him?'

This is how one parent responded to the challenge:

'Having comfortably ridden the early years with my son Jonathan, now aged ten, it was a tremendous shock one night to open my eyes in the middle of a prayer-time and to have my gaze squarely met by the two large round eyes of James, my three-year-old. He calmly announced: "I don't believe this Jesus thing ... I can't see him; I can't hear him; I can't feel him."

'Had he been older I could have dealt with that more easily. But, taking a deep breath, I explained that although he could not see, hear or feel me when I was downstairs, he knew I was there because I told him I was. And because I loved him, I would be there.

'Jesus has promised that, if we love him, he will be with us all the time. If he had a body like ours, he could only be in one place at a time. He couldn't keep his promise to all those people at once. We know he has kept his promise because we can talk to him and he answers our prayers.'

A teacher explained to her group of three- and four-year-olds who wanted to know why Jesus wasn't in at church:

'Jesus is always in at church, but we can't see him because he is in every church. If we could see him, he couldn't be in another church, or anywhere else at the same time. Jesus can be with us anywhere, not just at church – indoors and outside.'

Parents coming into church often say 'Sssh! This is God's house.' That can be a confusing statement to a young child. He might begin to wonder why God's house is not like his, why God isn't in, or 'Why do I have to be quiet – is God asleep?' The church, in fact, is no more God's house than your house is God's house. The word 'church' in the New Testament refers to 'God's people', not a building at all. The Bible says that God does not live in any building. God lives with his people and is not limited to one place.

Perhaps we could explain that a church is a special place used by Christians to worship God, to pray, sing and learn about him together. If there is a lot of noise, this may distract people from thinking about God. So it's good to be fairly quiet out of consideration for them.

Is Jesus God?
(seven-year-old)
Yes. Jesus said: 'The Father and I are one.'

Is God Jesus?
Yes. Jesus said: 'The Father is in me and . . . I am in the Father.'

Are there two Gods?
No. (See page 32.)

Why didn't God come to earth? Why did he send Jesus?
When God sent Jesus, he did come himself, but as a human being. We can't see or touch God. But the people who lived when Jesus was on earth were able to see him and touch him and listen to him as he taught them about God his Father. And Jesus said that anyone who had seen him had seen God.

By sending Jesus as a seed that grew into a baby then into a child, then into a man, who knew hunger, tears, happiness and sadness, God showed us himself in a way that we could understand. And because he sent Jesus, we know that God understands all about us. He's been one of us, so he can help us in all our troubles.

Why did Jesus have two dads?
(four-year-old)
God is Jesus' real dad. But Jesus had Joseph as his 'adopted' dad on earth so that he could live in a family like you.

For an older child the answer might be:
Jesus had Joseph as an earthly father to help look after him, his mother and brothers and sisters. But Jesus isn't just a

man. He is God's Son. And God his Father sent him to show us how to live and how we could become part of his family.

You could say you have two dads, too. We pray to God as 'our Father in heaven' and every one of us has a human father on earth.

Did Joseph mind when he found out Mary was pregnant before she was married?

(a seven-year-old, to her surprised grandmother)

I expect he did at first, but then God explained to him in a dream that the baby was very special. He was God's Son.

When the shepherds went to Bethlehem, who looked after the sheep?

(nine-year-old)

The Bible doesn't tell us that. Maybe a shepherd-boy stayed behind. But God certainly knew about them and would have made sure that they came to no harm.

How many people were healed by Jesus?

(nine-year-old)

A great many, though we don't know the exact number. We do know that he healed everyone who came to ask him. The Bible tells us about a lot of them.

Why did so many people hate Jesus?

(an eleven-year-old to his teacher)

People hated Jesus for lots of reasons. The Romans hated him because the Jews followed him in great crowds, and they thought he might lead a revolt. The Jewish priests hated him because he said he was God, and he pointed out how wrong they were. They were jealous that a carpenter should have so much knowledge and authority. Some people hated him just because he was so good: it made them feel uncomfortable.

Why didn't Jesus have Weetabix for breakfast instead of fish?

Why did Jesus forgive sins?

(eleven-year-old)

You know that when you've upset your parents or friends, there's bad feeling between you. But when you've said sorry and they've forgiven you, you are much happier and enjoy being with those people again. We've all done things we know God doesn't like. We've broken his rules. We've not lived up to his standards. He says we must love him with all our hearts, and that we must love other people. None of us has done that all the time. So we've spoiled our friendship with God. Jesus knows that the wrong things we do make us feel unhappy and guilty. So he offers to forgive us. He can 'wipe the slate clean' if we ask him and are truly sorry.

What would Jesus do to robbers and burglars?

(eleven-year-old)

Jesus would tell them they were doing wrong and hurting other people. He would want them to have the chance to change their way of life – to stop robbing and breaking into other people's houses, and to love and obey him instead.

Two robbers were crucified with Jesus. One just jeered at him, but the other asked Jesus' help and was forgiven.

* * *

The death and resurrection of Jesus are the core of the Christian message. But telling the story of the first Easter to children may present a number of problems.

Young children can be frightened by the story of the crucifixion. Some teachers disagree with it being taught and concentrate on a new life theme at Easter time; others feel that the spiritual understanding of a child must not be underestimated. The crucifixion story could be told from a historical point of view and emphasis put upon the resurrection.

One nursery teacher never teaches the crucifixion to children under eight:

'The four-year-old is struggling to come to terms with reality. Fact and fantasy are mixed together in his mind. For him to grasp the fact of a dead fly, worm, frog or guinea-pig is enough. Young children often poke at dead things, or shake them, to get them going again.

'So to talk to a four-year-old in terms of the meaning of the particular death of a certain man is futile. It is outside the scope of his mind and emotions.'

But sooner or later we have to answer the questions children ask:

Why did Jesus have to die?
What did he die on the cross for?
The story of Easter says Jesus died on the cross to save us from our sins, but how did that show God loves us?
(questions from seven-year-olds)

Jesus needn't have gone through with it. He could have stopped at any time, and he was tempted to do just that. But he loved us very much and he knew that the main reason for coming to earth was to rescue us. When he died, he suffered the punishment *we* deserved for all the wrong things we have done. He saved our lives – so that we can live as God's friends. It's a bit like a mum or dad jumping into a river to rescue their drowning child – even if it means they die instead. They do it because they love the child so much.

How did Jesus come alive again? You can't be dead one day and alive the next.
(seven-year-old)

'He could. He was God's Son. He was special!' answered her friend. (This might be sufficient for younger children.)

You're right. Dead people don't come back to life again. The fact that Jesus did is one of God's greatest miracles. Because God has made the laws which govern our world, he is able to use them for his own special purposes. He made the whole world from nothing! So he can even bring someone who is dead back to life. We don't know how he did it. But he had a very special reason. When he brought Jesus back to life, God was showing us that he had power over sin and death.

Was Jesus a ghost when he came alive again?
(seven-year-old)
No. After he had come alive again he went to see his friends. They thought at first that he was a ghost. But he said, 'Look at my hands and my feet, and see that it is I myself. Feel me and you will know, for a ghost doesn't have flesh and bones, as you can see I have.' He even ate some fish and had breakfast with them. Ghosts don't eat!

(N.B. Parents, beware of pictures that show Christ as 'ghost-like'. There are some 'horrors' and children may have got their ideas from these.)

Why did Jesus go back to heaven? Why can't he be on earth now?
He went back to heaven because he had finished the work that God had given him to do. He went to be with God his Father. And because he's no longer in just one place on earth he can help and be with all of us, everywhere.

He has promised to come back to earth one day. We don't know when that will be, but it's something to look forward to.

Is Jesus in every home?
(four-year-old)
He wants to be in every home, but only if people want him there. Jesus never pushes in where he is not wanted. If he is invited into a home, he always comes. He is in every home where the people love him.

If a special visitor comes to your front door, you wouldn't leave him standing there, would you? You, or Mummy or Daddy would go to the door and say, 'Come in'. Some people have never heard of Jesus; others may not understand that they must ask him to come into their lives; and some just can't be bothered to invite him.

(It might be helpful to show an older child the famous picture by Holman Hunt of Christ standing knocking at a door. There is no handle on the outside – the door can only be opened from the inside. This may help to explain that Jesus doesn't force his way in, but waits to be invited into someone's life.)

*   *   *

What's the Holy Ghost?

(seven-year-old)
The 'Holy Ghost' is the Spirit of Jesus/the Spirit of God. ('Ghost' is simply the old-English word for 'Spirit'.) He is God, just as Jesus is God. And he has special work to do. He is not a thing in a big white sheet, nor the scotch whisky sort of spirit! The Bible uses picture-language – wind, fire, a dove – to help us understand what the Holy Spirit is like.

Sometimes children have better answers to these questions than we do:

'He's the wind of God blowing the breath of Jesus all over the world.'
(a three-year-old)

'He helps me to understand Jesus. He points me to Jesus. He is the way that Jesus comes to all of us. He convinces people that Jesus is alive today.'
(a ten-year-old)

'He is my helper and guide through life. He comforts me and makes me joyful and peaceful. He helps me to know when I'm wrong.'
(a ten-year-old)

A definition from a family worship booklet says:

WILL MY RABBIT GO TO HEAVEN?

'He makes me more like Jesus, guides and strengthens me in my daily life, and helps me to serve God in the family of the church.'

How do you know he's there if you can't see him?
A teacher played a game with her class to illustrate this point. She made them all close their eyes, and explained that she was going to creep round the room and stand behind someone. When they thought she was behind their chair they could put up their hand. Some got it wildly wrong. Some got it right.

She asked the children, 'How did you know I was there?' And back came the answer: 'I felt you.'

She drew the parallel with the Holy Spirit (even though we don't 'feel' him), and also showed them how we 'see' him at work changing people's lives, answering prayer and helping us to overcome temper, jealousy and selfishness in our own lives.

*　　*　　*

Are God and Jesus and the Holy Spirit three people joined together, or one?
(eight-year-old)
This is a very difficult question to answer. I don't fully understand it myself.

Just think how parts of our bodies have different abilities: our eyes see, our ears hear, our legs walk. Each part is different, yet they all belong to the same person. So God, Jesus and the Holy Spirit have their separate work to do but are one person. Daddy is one person but he is also a father, a husband and a son. In each role he loves, helps and cares in a different way.

What are angels?
(three years and upwards)
They are messengers of God. The Bible gives a number of examples of God using angels to take messages to men and

THREE INTO ONE WILL GO

Tell me please, how can it be,
  God is one, and yet he's three?

Milk, tea, sugar, cup of tea,
  Three in one, and one in three.

Pea-pod, stalk, and small round pea,
  Three in one, and one in three.

Raindrops, rivers, mighty sea,
  Three in one, and one in three.

Trunk, leaves, branches, big green tree,
  Three in one, and one in three.

Mum and Dad and my baby,
  Three in one and one in three.

Father, Spirit, Son, though three,
  Still are one, and one in three.

women. It tells us that angels protect those who love God. The New Testament book of Hebrews says that angels are sent to serve people who love God.

What do they look like?

Sometimes they look like ordinary people. At the grave of Jesus on Easter morning, the women saw two angels. They described them as young men in bright shining clothes. Sometimes they appear in dreams to people, bringing a special message from God. An angel told Joseph in a dream about Mary's baby. Some people, like the shepherds in the fields near Bethlehem, were afraid when they saw angels, because they knew they had come from God himself. But the angels told them not to be afraid.

Do people become angels?

No! Angels are quite different from people.

Are they the same as fairies?

No! Fairies are 'pretend'. Angels are real.

Do you believe in guardian angels?

God uses his angels to guard and take care of his people. Some Christians believe in a guardian angel for each person. We don't really know that for certain but we can ask God to send his angels to protect us.

*   *   *

When do you pray?

(seven-year-old)

You can pray at any time and in any place. Often people have special times as well, like praying every day in the morning or the evening.

Why do you pray?

(five-year-old)

I need to say sorry, please and thank you to God. If I didn't talk

'What's all that chattering going on upstairs?'
'It's not us: it's our angels.'

to you, we wouldn't know each other very well, would we? So I need to talk to God in prayer to get to know him better. Jesus taught us to pray, to come to God as our Father. We can ask God to help us and to give us the things we need. Jesus prayed, so we need to pray as well.

Do you have to go to church to talk to God?
(nine-year-old)
No. You can talk to God anywhere at all. Jesus told us to go away on our own sometimes to be with God. It is easier to concentrate and think about God when we have peace and quiet. But Jesus also promised that when two or three of us are praying together, he will answer our requests. We can meet at church to pray with others, and it helps us to set time aside each week to do that.

How can you pray to someone you can't see?
(seven-year-old)
Praying is talking and listening. I can't see Gran when I'm on the telephone to her but I can speak to her and hear what she says to me.

How do you know God is listening?
He told us to pray, so of course he is going to listen. The Bible says that God is always more ready to listen and answer than we are to pray. The best way for you to find out and know for yourself is to try it. Then you will know.

How can you hear God's voice – is it like mine?
(six-year-old)
No, it isn't like our voices. It is a knowing-what-to-do inside you.

Does God really hear us when we pray?
(four-year-old, and upwards)
Yes. He wants us to talk to him. He always answers us, too.

Sometimes he says 'Yes', sometimes 'No', and sometimes 'Wait'.

Did people in Victorian times know about Jesus?
(nine-year-old)
Yes, they did! People in Britain had known about Jesus for hundreds of years by then. The Victorians were great churchgoers. But we don't know how many of them knew Jesus as a real person who could be with them, helping and guiding them every day. Some of them just believed they could go to church on Sundays and forget about Jesus and how he wanted them to live for the rest of the week.

How do we know the Bible is true?
There's a great deal of evidence that the Bible is historically true. There is more historical evidence for the existence of Jesus than for someone like Julius Caesar. We have the four Gospel accounts written soon after his death. And writings by non-Christian Roman historians called Suetonius and Tacitus and a Jewish historian called Josephus mention Jesus, too.

Discoveries by archaeologists confirm that the historical background of many stories in the Bible is correct. If you go to the British Museum in London or some of the other great museums, you can see copies of the Bible that are very, very old, and even fragments of New Testament books going back to within 100 years of when they were written.

The Bible has been investigated by more enquiring scholars than any other book in the world and it has stood the test of time.

Christians down the ages have proved the Bible's teaching to be true in their everyday life and experience.

The Bible is God's message to us: his 'word'. We know that God is a God of truth – why would he want to deceive us?

Some of the people who say they don't believe the Bible is true are really afraid of believing. They know that if they did, their lives would have to change.

How do you become a Christian?

A Christian is a follower of Jesus. Being good, going to church, even belonging to a Christian family doesn't make you a Christian. When Jesus called his first followers, they had to say 'yes' or 'no' to him. And we have to say 'yes' to become Christians.

From the time people first lived on earth, they have chosen to go their own way. They've done so many wrong things, it's as if a wall had been built between people and God. For God is completely just and good, so he can't just overlook sin and evil.

God sent his Son Jesus to break down the wall of wrong things and to make a way for everyone to come back to God. So, we have to admit the wrong things we have done, and accept that Jesus died for our wrongdoings (the death we deserved), so that God can forgive us.

Then we can thank Jesus for what he did and ask him to give us his new life and help us to be more like him from now on. Being a Christian does not mean we are any better than anyone else but that we are asking Jesus to help us live our lives as God wants.

Have you ever seen a pilot boat guiding a ship into a harbour? The harbour pilots know where the deep water channels are and can show the ship the safe way into port. Becoming a Christian is rather like handing over the control of the 'ship' of our life to Jesus, the 'pilot', and trusting him to show us the way to live.

What will happen to people who believed in God before Jesus came?

If they loved and obeyed God that's good enough for Jesus. He knows what's in their hearts. Although it's hard to understand, because Jesus is one with God, he has always been there, even before he came to earth as a man.

Do you have to go to church to be a Christian?

Going to church doesn't make you a Christian, but if you don't belong to a church, it's an awfully hard struggle being a Christian on your own. You need to meet with other Christians to worship God, pray and study the Bible together.

Life isn't going to go right all the time just because you are a Christian, and you need other Christians to help and encourage you. And other Christians in the church need you too. (It is the local group of Christians, not a particular kind of building, which is 'the church'.)

If you are a footballer, it's not much good playing lots of football on your own. You need to play in a team to enjoy the game fully, and contribute your skills to the team effort. Being a Christian is rather like that too. Individual Christians are like the parts of a human body – all the parts are necessary, and they must all work together for the whole body to function properly and healthily.

Why do we sing and talk in church about God giving us strength to fight all our battles, when we are not supposed to fight?

Those hymns and prayers are referring to the spiritual battle – it's not easy going God's way sometimes when we want to go our own way and it feels like a battle. It's not referring to physical battles.

What is sin?

Sin is pinching that chocolate biscuit Mum said you mustn't have until tomorrow. It's not allowing your friend to play with your toy train – and poking his eye when he does! In other words, sin is putting yourself first, and not behaving as God wants us to behave. Sin is 'missing the mark', like an archer who shoots off target. It means falling short of the standard God has set.

From newspapers, radio and television, we know about wars, murders, robberies and plenty of other ugly things

**Why do we have so many naughty people
around this place?**

which are the result of sin in the world. They are brought about by hatred, violence, greed and selfishness. And, if we're honest and look hard at ourselves, we can see wrong thoughts and actions in our lives, too. Sin is not just the bad things we do but also the good things we fail to do. An eleven-year-old put it this way: 'Sin is going against God's wishes.'

Why can't I sin?

You can. And we all do. But sin isn't fun, it's a spoilsport. It upsets our family life and our friendships, and makes us unhappy. Even worse, it cuts us right off from being friends with God because he can have nothing to do with it. Jesus can forgive us our sins and give us a fresh start, if we really want.

I wonder if God loves people who are bad and steal from shops?

A six-year-old replied to this question: 'God loves people who are bad but not what they have done wrong.'

*   *   *

Many children have friends from other religious backgrounds, and at school they will often be taught the meaning of some of the festivals of other major faiths. We should not shrink from this. It can be enriching for children, and can lead them from a giggling nervousness of the unfamiliar into a new respect for the beliefs and opinions of others.

But in the end they are bound to want to know if these beliefs are right. And if so, does that make Christians wrong?

It's an important question, as well as a hard one, because if children eventually conclude that all religions are equally true – just different ways of looking at the same thing – what we believe becomes simply a matter of personal preference.

Are the other religions true?

Christians believe that God sent Jesus to show us what he is like, and to die so that everyone who believes in him can be forgiven for their wrongdoings and live with him for ever. So a Christian has to say that anything in other religions which teaches us that God is different from the way Jesus showed him, or that there is some other way to be forgiven, is wrong. But the things in other religions which don't go against Jesus' teaching may well be true, even if the words and practices seem strange to us.

(This answer leaves many questions unresolved. But it is the approach that will help us to preserve in our children both an openness to the light of God wherever they find it, and faith in Jesus as the truth by which all other teaching about God is measured.)

Are the other gods real?

There is only one God who made the world and is in control of everything, who loves and cares for us. The Bible makes it plain that other 'gods' are just man-made images with no real life or power.

2

Questions about death and suffering

'You've been feeling tired,' said the stranger, 'but I can do something about that. I've come to ask whether you'd care to join my Owsla. We shall be glad to have you and you'll enjoy it. If you're ready, we might go along now.'

They went out past the young sentry, who paid the visitor no attention. The sun was shining and in spite of the cold there were a few bucks and does at silflay, keeping out of the wind as they nibbled the shoots of spring grass.

It seemed to Hazel that he would not be needing his body any more, so he left it lying on the edge of the ditch . . .

From *Watership Down*, by Richard Adams

Does God take the flowers on the coffin?

What happens when you die?'

You stop living!

Does God read the messages on the coffin?

Daddy won't need his glasses any more. He can see now.

'... and the nicest thing always comes at the end, like going to heaven. Being born is rather squashy, but going to heaven is beautiful. I always think it is like eating cabbage for dinner. Awful. I always eat that first (or at least I try) and save the nicest thing till last.'
(a five-year-old)

When animals die, why does God make them into clouds?

It's better being a human when you die than an animal because you get eternalised but animals get pulverised.

My Grandad died of a heart attack and when I go upstairs I always think that I am next and someone is going to stab me in the back. On the day that he died he always comes back into my bedroom.

Why has Daddy been buried without his feet?

Why do you ask that?

Because you said his soul had gone to heaven.

'It's no good, Grannie, Grandad is dead. You'll just have to get on living without him.'
(a practical six-year-old, trying to comfort his grandmother!)

Where do dogs go when they die? They don't go down the toilet like goldfish do.

Young children appear to accept death more easily than adults. Most of them are also ready and eager to talk about it, unlike some of their elders who view it, nowadays, as a taboo subject. Children will enact it, question it and, on occasions, express their fear of it. Some, however, may be afraid to ask and need to be encouraged not to keep their fears and questions to themselves.

We need to be careful of language and understanding difficulties, avoiding if possible the old clichés when discussing death with our children. It is not always helpful to suggest that 'God has taken Grandad', because God could then be viewed as a 'kidnapper' who whisks people away. Similarly, 'Grandma has gone to Jesus' can suggest that Grandma didn't like us and preferred Jesus' company.

One mother had to tell her children, Richard (eight), Margaret (seven) and Gill (five), that Auntie Rose had died after a long illness. The older two were quiet and upset, as she had been a great favourite, but Gill kept on giggling, until Richard became cross and asked Mum to tell her how naughty she was. Wisely, Mum waited until she was alone with Gill. Then she asked why Gill had laughed.

'Well,' replied Gill, 'my Sunday school teacher told us that when we die our body stays here and we go to heaven.'

'Yes,' said her Mum.

'Well, I think we must look funny with our arms and legs stuck on our heads – and I was thinking how funny Auntie Rose would look!' Gill explained.

How easily we say things – forgetting that the 'body' is often the 'trunk' to a child.

Just think of the number of children who conduct proper funerals for the dead bird they find, or their beloved guinea-pig.

'Where are you going with that lot?' Mum asked, seeing her two children (eight and six) wandering along with a trowel, a shoe-box, a bundle of crumpled feathers and an old prayer-book.

'To bury this poor little bird in a coffin and sing so he can go to Jesus,' replied the younger child cheerily.

Often a child's first experience of death is through a dead animal such as a pet – and this may help in explaining the death of a relative or friend when the occasion arises. It's obvious to them that when it's dead, the pet no longer breathes or feels. Holding up a dead mouse, a three-year-old was heard to remark, 'No more good, won't go any more.'

Will my rabbit be in heaven when he dies?

(nine-year-old)
God created the animals and he put us in charge of them. God cares for all his creation and Jesus told us that God cares about every little bird that falls to the ground dead. So we can trust him to look after your rabbit when he dies.

What happened to Grandad's dog?

(six-year-old)
He died. He grew very old and couldn't run any more. He couldn't enjoy life either and his body just wore out. He died, with Grandad near him, knowing how much he was loved.

Grandad can't run any more either – will he die too? Why do people die?

(four-year-old)
Usually people die when they are old and tired. Their bodies get worn out, just as old clothes get worn out. So yes, Grandad will die some day. When that happens it will be time for him to leave his old body, and go to live with Jesus in heaven. (This will probably satisfy a four-year-old; for an older child, a longer answer might be needed.)

There is always somebody dying, just as there is always somebody being born. Some people die when they are young because they get very ill, or because they have an accident in which their body is badly damaged. The Bible says that for

*Why did my budgie die? You must know if I do
not know. He was just getting used to me. I
hope you are taking care of him, and I hope
you are taking care of my cat and dog . . .
and dear God please look after my
great-grandfather who died too.*

everyone there is a time to live and a time to die. And God knows the right time for each person.

Does everyone go to heaven when they die?

Everyone who loves and follows Jesus can be sure that they will go to heaven when the time comes for them to die. But God doesn't force people to live with him in heaven if they don't want to. We can choose.

What happens to you when you die?

Think what happens when you move house. You leave the building behind and take with you all that matters from inside it. Your body is like a house containing all the important things inside it. When we die, we leave our old bodies behind because they are now of no use to us. And we take what's really important, the real you and me, with us. Just as snakes shed their old skins, so we shed our old bodies when we die and our real selves go to heaven.

Have you ever watched a caterpillar? Do you know that it turns into a beautiful butterfly? That's very like our lives. While we live on earth we are like the caterpillar. We are concerned with eating and sleeping to keep our bodies alive, but the best part is still to come. When we die, we leave behind our old bodies (like the caterpillar when it becomes a chrysalis). Then the real part of us that lived in our bodies is given a beautiful new body for the life with God – like the caterpillar becoming a butterfly.

If God gives us life, why do people die?

(ten-year-old)

When God made the world, it wasn't part of his plan for people to die. Death is ugly and unnatural. God told the first people they would die if they disobeyed his command. They chose to ignore what he said. And so death came into the world. But even then God had planned a way for people to live. He sent Jesus to offer people 'eternal life', as his gift. For all who accept his gift, death is not the end. It's just the gateway to a new life with him.

I would like to ask Jesus if death worried him? He'd probably say no, but I'm worried, if he asks me.

(eleven-year-old)

Although Jesus came to earth to die for us, he asked God, if it were possible, to spare him that terrible pain and suffering. So he knows what it is like to be worried about dying and he can help us. We don't need to worry about what will happen after we die, because if we love Jesus we know that we'll be safe and happy with him.

Does everyone die when they go to hospital?

(a seven-year-old to his mum, as she was about to go into hospital)

No, of course not. Hospitals are there to make people better. Most people get well and go home. All the time doctors and nurses are learning more and more about making people better. A long time ago, there were no hospitals and many people did die when they were very ill. Sometimes, if someone is very old and their body has worn out, or if they are very ill and their body isn't working properly, they die in hospital. Or if someone's body is very badly damaged in an accident and cannot be made better, they may die in hospital.

Why are people put in the earth? Won't they get cold in this weather?

(a six-year-old, on a frosty morning)

It doesn't matter about the cold. When you die, your body doesn't feel pain or heat or cold any more. Your body is put in the ground where it becomes part of the soil. If you love Jesus, the bit that is 'you' – the part that feels, thinks and loves – goes to be with him.

Will my baby brother have a little box or a big one when he dies?

Usually people don't die until they are grown-up, old, and their bodies are worn out. If, sadly, a baby is ill and his body isn't working properly, then he may die and, yes, he would be put in a little coffin.

When will I die?

Not for a long, long time. Everyone has to die sometime, but nobody knows when. Usually it happens when you are very old.

Do you go straight to heaven when you die?

Yes. Jesus told the thief who was hanging on a cross beside him when he was dying: 'I promise you that today you will be in Paradise with me.'

When you die, do you become a ghost?

No. In heaven we shall have special, new bodies as Jesus did when he came back to life. We shan't grow old, or be ill or in pain.

Why do people send flowers at funerals?

People give flowers to show their love and affection for the person who has died and for the relatives left behind. Not everybody wants to have flowers at funerals and sometimes, before they die, they, or their relatives, suggest that the money that would have been spent on flowers goes to a charity instead.

Why do people ride in black cars at funerals?

(seven-year-old)

Why do they wear black at funerals?

It's been the custom for centuries in the Western world for people to wear black. In parts of China and in Africa and other countries, they wear white or purple. Black isn't really a 'colour' at all. So it seemed to suit sorrowful or sombre occasions, as bright colours suited festive occasions. Black not only showed the sorrow of the relatives or friends of the dead person, but it was a reminder to others that someone close to them had died. People could then be careful not to say anything upsetting to them. Black cars, like black clothes, were chosen to suit the occasion.

Some Christians ask people to wear bright colours to their funerals, because death to them means a new life with God. So it's a festive occasion, even though their friends are sad to lose them.

Why do people cry at funerals?

They cry because they are sad at the thought of not seeing again the person who has died. Christians know that one day they will see each other again in heaven. But, even so, it makes them sad to know that they are parted in the meantime. It is good to cry and show our grief. That helps us to feel better about it, to accept that the person has died, and to let our feelings show, instead of bottling them up inside us. Jesus was not ashamed to cry when his friend Lazarus died.

Do you want to be buried or fired?

(seven-year-old to his mum)

'I want to be cremated,' she answered. 'That's what you mean when you say "fired". Being cremated at a special place called the crematorium saves the ground being used up! I shall have a new body when I go to heaven, so I won't need this old one, and it might as well be disposed of as quickly and neatly as possible! Some people prefer to be buried and the relatives sometimes like to visit the grave.'

Can I have your jewellery and Cliff Richard records when you are dead?

(nine-year-old)
In the event, burglars got there first! So a lesson was learnt – by Mum, too – about not trusting in material possessions!

*　　*　　*

But some practical questions about death cannot be avoided, especially if a close relative is involved.

'Does Granny have eyes in heaven?' asked a three year-old, and she went on asking similar questions for nights on end. To her mother this was very painful. Although Granny had been ill for some time, it nevertheless came as a shock when she finally died. Her daughter (the three-year-old's mother) was surprised at her own reaction and the grief it caused her. To make matters worse, the child's questions always came at bedtime when they were both tired.

'At the time my husband was the same age at which my father had died so I was anxious about him as well. I just did not know how to cope with these awful questions. Finally I was so worn down by them that I sought help.'

She went to a naval captain who was experienced in counselling the bereaved and those facing tragedies in their lives. He explained that the child was afraid that now Granny had gone, she herself might die and Mummy might go too. He advised the mother not to tackle the questions at night, but to choose a time when she felt she could sit down with her daughter and reassure her. This she did, and the questions stopped. The fear had been removed.

She explained that normally, we live out our lifespan and that this is God's wish and plan for us. We are born, develop through childhood to adult life and into old age until our bodies are worn out and we are ready to die. 'You won't die, Mummy, will you?' needs to be answered in very reassuring terms for the fearful child, who is anxious not only about losing Mum, but about how he'll manage without her.

One Dutch father reassured his sobbing little girl in this way:

'When you and I go to Amsterdam – when do I give you the ticket?'

'Why, just before we get on the train,' answered the child.

'Exactly ... and our wise Father in heaven knows when we're going to need things, too. Don't run out ahead of him. When the time comes that some of us will have to die, you will look into your heart and find the strength you need – just in time.' (From *The Hiding Place*, by Corrie ten Boom.)

Children often have questions in their minds they find difficult to put into words and they need to feel free to discuss all their feelings.

A child might worry because he doesn't actually feel grief for a close member of the family who has died, especially if he hasn't known them very well and may need reassurance that he need not feel guilty about this.

This is how another child felt: 'All I can remember about my first experience of death in the family was a feeling of being left out of something important, something I was supposed to be crying about.'

And just to remind us that children do not think the way we do, there was the child who asked, while walking through a cemetery, 'What are those big stones for?' When told that they marked the place where people had been buried, she replied, 'Do they hurt the people underneath?'

This is matched by the four-year-old who was found digging a hole in the garden a week after the funeral of his elder brother. His parents heard him shout down the hole, 'Dan, can you hear me? What are you doing?'

*   *   *

The death of a parent raises all kinds of questions in children's minds. Children who have lost one parent are likely to be anxious about losing the other. A question like 'You're not old, Mummy, are you?' needs to be met with special reassurance. The following questions, from four- to eight-year-olds, reveal some other fears which need calm and sensitive handling.

What will happen to Daddy's/Mummy's body?

If it's been buried, after a long time it will become part of the soil again. If it's been cremated, the body and bones are burnt so that there's only a little heap of ash left.

But what happens to the body can't hurt the person once they are dead. The body is only a 'shell'. The real person isn't inside it any more.

Where is Daddy/Mummy?
Is he with God?
Is he happy?
Can he see us?
Does he miss us?

Daddy/Mummy has died. Because he loved God, he's with God in heaven now. He's very happy and he's well. He's not ill or in pain any more. He's not in our time-world any more, so he won't have time to miss us. We'll see him again when we go to heaven, and to Daddy that will seem no time at all. I'm sure he knows all about us. He hasn't stopped loving and caring for us.

How can God be kind if he doesn't give our daddy back?

God is kind. He doesn't want us to be unhappy. He's loving us with an extra-special love just now, because he knows how much we miss Daddy. But we couldn't wish Daddy to be ill again. It's best for him to be with God.

What about my airfix model we were making? I thought I was going to do all sorts of things with Dad, like trains and making aeroplanes.

We all miss Daddy's help. He did such a lot for us. But he

wouldn't want us to be miserable. He'd want us still to do all the things he'd planned for us. Let's ask Uncle John if he'll help with the model.

Why don't you marry David's daddy? I don't want to live without a daddy for years and years.

We can't find another daddy just like that! There are other people missing their dad or mum just like us. And we know that God will help us. We have only to ask him. And perhaps he will send us another daddy at some time in the future.

Will we see Daddy's ghost?

No. We don't become ghosts when we die. When someone dies and goes to be with God, you don't see them any more. Daddy wouldn't want to frighten you, would he?

Why did my baby brother die?

(The answer to this will obviously depend on the circumstances in which baby died and also on the age of the child to whom the answer is being given. A purely factual answer may be all that is required, although an older child may really be asking 'Why did God *let* my baby brother die?')

He was born before his body was strong enough to live/He was very ill (or whatever the *physical* reason was). People don't usually die when they are babies. Our baby is well and happy now with God. We will see him again when we go to heaven. And maybe God will give us another baby one day.

Why did my baby sister die?

An old lady, answered this question: 'What would heaven be like without any children?'

A six-year-old answered his own question by saying: 'I know why – God made a mistake! She was so beautiful he took her back again.'

*　　*　　*

When it comes to tackling questions about suffering, we need to admit right away that we do not understand and do not have all the answers. Jesus never fully explained it, but he did alleviate it.

We need to emphasize that God doesn't promise to remove difficulties, but he does promise us his help to cope with them. The apostle Paul begged God to take away an affliction he had, but God's answer was, 'My grace is enough for you'.

Why isn't Gran better? I asked God to make her.
Perhaps Gran is getting better slowly but we are too impatient to see it. Or, perhaps Gran is very old and her body has worn out so she is ready to die and go to live with God in heaven.

Why did God let my mum die?
Perhaps he didn't want her to suffer any more pain. We don't understand why some things happen because we can't possibly see the whole of God's plan. But we do know that God is loving and good. Life is rather like a jigsaw puzzle: God has the finished picture but we only see the pieces fitting in as we go along. Sometimes it is hard to see how some pieces do fit in, but we know that God's plan is best.

Nice things and nasty things happen to everyone. What is important is our reaction to what happens to us. We learn through hard times to be brave and strong. We all have to die at some time or other. But Jesus has gone back to God to get a place ready for us in heaven. With him there is no more pain or sadness. So there is no need for those left behind to worry. Jesus takes care of them, too, and will make sure they are looked after.

Are you unlucky to get ill like this?
(five-year-old whose mum has cancer)
The simple, general answer to this question might be:
    No, everyone gets ill sometimes. You've had mumps,

Grandad's got flu and the baby has a cold. Usually the illnesses are not very bad and people get better quickly. Sometimes people get bad illnesses, like cancer, which involve having a lot of treatment, going to hospital for a while and having to rest in bed more often than they usually do.

The whole question of terminal or severely disabling disease, and the problem of helping a young child to face or accept the death of a parent, brother or sister, is extremely complex.

'Are you unlucky to get ill like this?' What is the child really asking?

Between the ages of two and seven, a child begins to be a thinking creature. But he lacks experience and so lacks scientific logic. He sees his parents as God. The morality he knows is an authoritarian one. If he is naughty, he is punished (something unpleasant happens). If something unpleasant happens, it therefore follows that he must have been naughty. Conscience is emerging and is a new source of anxiety.

So there are two 'load words' in the question. The first is 'unlucky'. The thought in the child's mind may be: 'Has God picked on you, Mummy?' 'Have I been naughty, so is God punishing me?' 'Did you choose to get cancer in order to punish me because I am so naughty?' 'Is it anything to do with me?'

The second load word is 'cancer'. Does the child know that cancer can be fatal? Does he fear it always is – now or later? What is the time-scale? Is he aware of the concern in the family group? Is he sensitive to the reactions of some members in the group, leading to fear of the disease? Is he angry that it has come? Is he jealous of the attention given to his mother?

Emotions of these kinds can be going on in a five-year-old in this situation, and have to be dealt with by an adult. In this case, the shortest and simplest answer will not necessarily do. It isn't like a sex question, where a point of information only is being asked for. This is an experience the child is trying to evaluate. It may take some time. The adult would have to listen carefully and watch the child at play, to discover which particular emotion is the main problem. Professional advice can also be obtained in helping children to face up to this situation.

Having explained about illnesses, bad and not so bad, the child could be told that some illnesses, like cancer, are dangerous.

'Cancer can make people die. Sometimes the doctors can stop it, and sometimes they can't. It is very sad that I have cancer, and it is frightening. I feel frightened, and maybe you do as well. We don't know why I have to get cancer, or why anyone does. Everyone has to cope with some sort of suffering in their life – and for some people it is worse than for others.

'We don't know exactly what is going to happen. We do know that there are people – doctors, nurses and friends – who will help us as much as they can. And we do know that God still loves me and still loves you.'

If the child does have to face up to the death of his mother, honesty is essential. Pain must be acknowledged. A child must feel free to show sadness and to cry. Acceptance of emotions is very important. The mother may want to prepare the child herself along these lines, if her death becomes certain:

'We know that if I do have to die, God will still take care of me and keep me near to him. He will also take care of you and send you someone to look after you properly. It will be very sad and you will want to cry. But you won't go on being unhappy for ever. Later on you will feel better. You'll know that I want you to be happy and enjoy all the good things there are, even if I can't be with you.'

(The author wishes to acknowledge the help given by the

book *Children Under Stress* by Sulu Wolff in answering this particular question.)

* * *

Why is my sister a spastic? I hate God!
Why did God not love me and make me spina bifida?
Why should I say thank you to him?

God does love you. You are very special to him. When he sees people hurting he cares about them very much. He didn't make you to have spina bifida. His plan is for each of us to be whole people and not have anything wrong. Sometimes things do go wrong with our bodies when we are growing inside our mothers. We don't always know why that happens but we do know that God cares, and knows how we feel. He has promised that when we go to live with him in heaven we shall have new bodies which are perfect. There will be no more pain, disease, old age or handicap.

It's how we react to handicap and disability that's inportant. We can let it make us bitter and spoil our lives or we can take the problem to God who has his own plan for every life. He often gives special gifts to handicapped people. They can teach those who are well things they might not learn otherwise – to look after other people, not to be sorry for themselves, to be brave, or just to be who they are . . . We can love God and please him whether we're well or ill. Those are the things that matter. We don't have to thank him for spina bifida, but we can thank him for helping us to cope with it; for those who look after us, and for his love.

What's wrong with that man over there?
Why are there so many people here in wheelbarrows?

Answering questions about handicap is not easy – partly because we may not have the correct information and also for fear of hurting the person concerned, particularly when a child asks directly within earshot, or stares, long and hard.

Most handicapped people will not mind if a *child* stares or ask questions. In the right circumstances it may be possible to encourage them to ask the handicapped person about their condition.

Many organizations and societies are encouraging communities to be far more understanding and accepting of handicapped people in general. If children can be encouraged to smile and communicate naturally with them, from an early age, so much the better for everyone.

Meeting with an adult or child who is mentally or physically handicapped (sometimes they are both) provides a good opportunity to talk about it later, encouraging the children's questions so that they can understand a little better next time. It's a moment, too, for emphasizing that there is no perfect human being. None of us has a perfectly ordered body or mind – able to do everything. Each of us is handicapped or disabled in some way. But some people have the misfortune through illness, accident or being born with a disability to appear more severely handicapped than others.

Why is Lisa handicapped?

This is a natural question for young children to ask about handicapped friends. We will need to find out about the handicap or disability from the parent/teacher or an organization, in order to give an informative explanation.

This is how the organization MENCAP defines mental handicap:

'It is a permanent disability which can happen in any family. A mentally handicapped child is born with a brain which will not develop as fast or function as well as a normal child's.

'There are many causes, most of which we don't yet fully understand. We know that Down's Syndrome (mongolism) is caused by an extra chromosome; that a baby's brain can be damaged at birth; that German measles during pregnancy can result in a mentally handicapped baby; and so on.

'But often we can't fully explain how or why it happened.'

Physical handicap is easier to explain. It is when parts of the body are damaged, missing or deformed. Or when the brain fails to get messages to the various parts of the body.

'Ere, your legs are behaving badly again today, aren't they?' said one exasperated six-year-old able-bodied child, trying to help an equally exasperated handicapped child.

Most of the organizations and societies will give information and encourage the membership of able-bodied people. At last the benefits of integrated education are beginning to be understood, and nurseries, playgroups and primary schools are now taking children with handicaps which would previously have meant them going to special schools.

Why am I not a running boy? Am I broken?

The reason you are not a 'running boy' is not because you are broken but because the nerves in your spine are not working properly and your legs won't run for you. But there's so much you can do. And we love you, and so does God.

Why I be stupid? Why does my teacher give me a pencil that goes 'do lally' and the other children pencils that write on lines?

You are not stupid, and it's not the pencil that's different. It's just that your brain is unable to get a message through to your fingers quickly enough to tell them how to hold the pencil correctly. But we'll work at it together. There are people who can't hold a pencil at all, and that's not because they're stupid either. There are many clever things you *can* do.

Will God give me another arm if I hurt this one?

No, you wouldn't get another arm but it could be mended if it wasn't hurt too badly. Some people are given artificial arms. Our bodies are complicated machines, so we need to look after them – and other people's too.

Can handicapped people swim?
Can handicapped people go in aeroplanes like me?

Yes, many handicapped people can swim, some of them very well indeed. They love the feeling of being in water because they can move more easily. They take part in lots of sports and hold their own competitions and Olympics. It's great fun to race in a wheelchair, or play hockey in one.

They can go in aeroplanes for holidays like you and can enjoy ski-ing, climbing and riding. But it costs money and we all need to do what we can so that more handicapped people can have holidays and opportunities like these.

Why do they have handicapped people in this country?

It has nothing to do with the country you live in – unless you are thinking about the unfortunate people who are caught up in accidents like the one that occurred in the Russian nuclear power station or those in India who were blinded by poisonous chemicals escaping into the environment. Every country has handicapped people. There are people in the Third World countries who are handicapped through starvation and not enough of the right things to eat. We must do all we can to look after our nation and help others to use their land and resources properly, to help prevent handicap.

Why can't those children eat properly?

(This was asked after seeing a programme on television and also after a Christmas party, organized by MENCAP.)
Why can't he hold his knife and fork?
When will he be able to feed himself?

Do you remember when your brother was a baby and he had to be fed – what a messy eater he was to begin with? There are some children who may look the same age as you but have minds and bodies that work only as well as a baby's or a very young child's. This makes it extremely difficult for them to learn how to eat. They are unable to remember to keep their mouths closed – even you forget that sometimes! Other children may know how to feed themselves but, because their brains are not working as they should, cannot control their arms, hands and fingers. If you think about it, eating is a very complex activity – it involves so many parts of you.

Children can find it difficult to distinguish between sickness which they experience and handicap. They may ask: 'Are you born handicapped or can you catch it?' 'Why do people make children handicapped?' We can reassure them that it is perfectly safe to cuddle handicapped people. You can't catch handicap like a cold or chickenpox.

3

Questions about heaven and the other place

The Unicorn . . . stamped his right fore-hoof on the ground . . . : 'I have come home at last! This is my real country! I belong here. This is the land I've been looking for all my life, though I never knew it till now. The reason why we loved the old Narnia is that it sometimes looked a little like this.'

All of them passed in through the golden gates, into the delicious smell that blew towards them out of that garden and into the cool mixture of sunlight and shadow under the trees, walking on springy turf that was all dotted with white flowers. The first thing that struck everyone was that the place was far larger inside than it had seemed from the outside.

Aslan turned to them and said:

'You do not yet look as happy as I mean you to be.'

Lucy said, 'We're so afraid of being sent away, Aslan . . .'

'No fear of that,' said Aslan, '. . . all of you are – as you used to call it in the Shadowlands – dead. The term is over: the holidays have begun. The dream is ended: this is morning.'

From *The Last Battle*, by C. S. Lewis

Do all worn-out grannies go to heaven?

Why do people dress up at Halloween like witches to scare the people and the babies?

Can brooms fly?

Is God a wizard?

Do goblins come out at Halloween?

How does God cope with all them people up there in heaven?

'Saints are people who let the light shine through.'
(five-year-old)

I think God is like an angel.
He is kind, dressed up in white robes
with long brown hair. He forgives our
sins. He has a kind smiling face. He
lives in heaven above the universe
and I think it's like white clouds mixed
together.

I think I will go to heaven
tomorrow. Will that be
all right?

Do we have wings
to fly to heaven?

You don't have to be a small child to ask questions about heaven. A question may come from an inquiring five-year-old, or from his intelligent grandfather who freely admits he would love to know heaven as a 'real place'.

The Russian cosmonaut on his journey in space may have been surprised not to find God 'up there'. But Christians today don't really believe that heaven is quite literally 'above the bright blue sky', as the hymn puts it.

In attempting to describe heaven, many have tried to explain it as a different world altogether, using poetic imagery. Children tend, without prompting, to think of heaven, where God lives, as 'above', and hell, where the devil lives, as 'below'.

A three-year-old, in reply to his mum's command to eat up his lunch, said, 'No, God has not told me to eat up my dinner. He isn't looking through his hole in the sky at me. He doesn't do that until it's dark.'

As he grows older, his mum will need to explain that we can't really think of heaven as a place with a single, definable location. For if we don't help children to understand this, they may grow up to dismiss the whole of Christianity as a fairy-tale. Especially when astronauts fail to find God in the heavens!

In the book of Revelation in the Bible, the apostle John describes his vision of a new earth and a new heaven. In his *Narnia Chronicles*, particularly *The Last Battle*, C. S. Lewis provides his own beautiful description of what heaven is like. Reading this – preferably aloud – a child (or a grown-up) can catch a glimpse of heaven at whatever level of spiritual understanding they, as individuals, have reached.

One mum asked her seven-year-old daughter what she would wish for if she had three wishes. The child thought. Then Mum explained that her own three wishes would be no more fighting or war; no more suffering or pain; no more hunger or disease.

Mum then showed her daughter the part of Revelation

chapter 21 in which heaven is seen as a place where 'there will be no more death, no more grief or crying or pain', for God will be with his people and 'will wipe away all tears from their eyes'.

She encouraged the child to think how she would describe a fantastic place, somewhere far better than anything she had ever known, and then to read some verses of John's vision in that chapter of Revelation. She explained how difficult it is for us to imagine heaven – or anything else which is completely outside our experience (space going on for ever and ever; life on other planets; or creatures in a different form from those known to us).

If a simpler answer is required for a younger child, the picture-language used by Jesus (John's Gospel, chapter 14) of a house with rooms especially prepared for us, might help.

A nursery teacher felt it enough to explain to her four-year-olds that heaven is where all the friends of Jesus go when they die.

A parent gave this answer to her seven year-old: 'How do you feel when Mummy or Daddy is away? To be away from God is like that. That warm, safe feeling you have when you are together with Mummy and Daddy is the sort of feeling you can have all your life if you belong to God. Being with God after we leave behind the bodies we have on earth is to be in heaven. The wonderful thing is that we can begin to have some idea of what that will be like right now if we love Jesus and try to follow him.'

Another said, 'Imagine heaven as a world where no one ever does wrong or even thinks wrong thoughts. It is perfect. It's how God wanted the world to be in·the beginning, but it was spoiled by people's selfishness and disobedience.'

Is heaven above space?
(seven-year-old)
No. Heaven is where God is, and he doesn't live in one particular place.

God, why did my fish die? I loved them so much.
I had fourteen of them. Can you tell me where
my fish are? Are they in heaven or in hell?

Do you sit around all day in heaven? I don't want to get bored.

(eight-year-old)

You don't get bored being with your friends and with people you love, do you? Heaven is being with Jesus and, if we love him, we'll be looking forward to seeing him and being with him. I'm sure God's prepared lots of things for us to do that we can't even imagine now.

Will we have Smarties, Hershey, Mars bars ... all the things we want in heaven?

I'm sure we'll have all we want. I expect we'll be so excited and happy that we won't even think about things like our favourite sweets or candies! God will have so much for us to enjoy. He will make sure that everyone is happy.

Am I good enough to go to heaven or too naughty?

(eleven-year-old)

It's just as well we don't get to heaven by being good, or the place would be empty! No one is good enough for God, however many good things they do. We can only get to heaven by trusting Jesus and by living his way. We are able to go to heaven because Jesus died on the cross, taking the punishment for the wrong things we've done, and came alive again. He makes it all possible for us to know and love God personally and to believe that God knows and loves us just as we are.

When I go to heaven, can I see Grandad?

(nine-year-old)

Yes. The Bible says we shall have special new bodies to replace our earthly bodies and we shall be able to recognize people.

Why doesn't God teleport us up to heaven, so I can see Gran?
(six-year-old)
(It's tempting to reply that Gran would probably like a bit of peace and quiet for a while!)
People don't go to heaven and come back! It isn't a place somewhere out in space. And there are no buses or trains or 'liberators' to take us there. We can only go there when we die – then we'll see Gran again.

Now Uncle Bill is in heaven, can I ask him to tell me what it is like?
(eight-year-old)
No. God doesn't let us speak to people who have died. They are in his care and he looks after them. He has told us as much about heaven as we can understand now.

Now Grandad is in heaven, is he young again?
Grandad has a new and different sort of body in heaven: one without aches and pains or anything wrong with it. I don't think we could say he's 'young' or 'old' in the way we can about people here on earth.

*   *   *

Questions about heaven are going to lead to questions about hell. If previous questions haven't brought problems, these certainly will!

Few of us want to talk about hell, yet most children have gleaned snippets about it – maybe in the form of threats from the older generation! They may have the idea of a place populated with lurid creatures with horns, tails and a pitchfork. They may describe gleefully, or fearfully, the flames of hell and the torments people suffer there.

Do we ignore all this, or deal with it? We may well find ourselves faced with questions like: 'Is hell the place where

Jesus won't give the people any water?' 'Is it hot? Is there fire and brimstone?' 'Will wicked people go to hell?' 'What's going to happen to me when I die?' (This last question was also asked by an intelligent, mature teacher still haunted by the images placed in her mind as a child and revived by a television programme on Satan worship.)

It's better to talk of hell in terms of separation from God, rather than somewhere hot, or indeed a place at all. Some people could be described as being in 'hell' now – being burnt up inside by anger, hatred, jealousy, bitterness and resentment. Just as heaven can be described as 'where God is' and can be experienced in people's lives now, so hell is the state of being cut off from God and equally can begin here and now.

If someone is very ill in hospital and they are evil and then they die, will they go to hell?
(eight-year-old)
Not everyone who is ill in hospital is going to die. Most people get well and go home. We cannot know what people are really like – only God can know that. Even when they are so ill that they can't speak to us or understand what we say to them, I'm sure God can get through to them. If they are really sorry for the wrong things they have done and they ask God to forgive them, he will. While we are alive, it is never too late to ask God for forgiveness. Jesus told one of the thieves who was dying on a cross beside him that he would be with Jesus in 'paradise', or heaven.

What does the devil look like?
We don't really know what he looks like. The pictures we see are only artists' impressions, trying to portray something nasty, evil and horrible. But the Bible says that he can assume many different forms: a serpent, a roaring lion, the spirit who controls people who disobey God. He may even appear in disguise as an 'angel of light'.

Most adults try to explain Satan as an evil force, an 'enemy of God' whom we can't see but whose influence and power we feel in our lives. C. S. Lewis clearly depicts the forces of good and evil in his book *The Lion, the Witch and the Wardrobe*. And the film *Star Wars* also takes up this theme.

Children may be frightened of the devil, and we need to emphasize that they are safe and secure in Jesus.

If we can't see him how do we know he is there? Has anybody seen the devil?

We may not have seen the devil but we can see the effects of his activity in the world: war, cruelty, greed, selfishness and all kinds of unhappiness. We are aware of him in our own lives, tempting us to think and to do what is wrong. Sometimes a voice in our minds tells us to do wrong and unkind things: 'Go and hit him', 'Don't do what Mum tells you', "There's no need to say sorry', 'Aren't you feeling miserable today?' (instead of being thankful for what you have), 'You want that? Well, you go and get it! Never mind anyone else.' We can be sure that the devil puts these thoughts in our minds. Jesus knew the devil was real because he was tested by him in the wilderness.

How do I know whether the voices in my mind are God, the devil, or me just thinking things?

(Mum sympathized with this question; she has the same difficulty!)

Ask yourself what those inside 'voices' are saying. Is it the kind of thing that God or the devil would say? Usually the devil puts doubts in our mind, questions God's commands and tempts us to think, say or do wrong and unkind things.

God's 'voice' is usually heard comforting and reassuring us, telling us he loves us, encouraging us to follow him, to turn away from wrong, guiding us and challenging us to serve him in the world.

*   *   *

Are there witches nowadays?

If asked by a young child, this question probably refers to old hags in pointed hats who ride on broomsticks and put nasty spells on people. The answer in that case is a definite 'no'. Those sorts of witches are only in storybooks.

Until quite recently, people who lived lonely, slightly unusual lives were often accused of being witches and were feared because they were misunderstood. This reply would have been sufficient for an older child prior to the recent upsurge of interest in the occult. The situation has changed dramatically, and today there are people who deliberately devote their lives to sorcery and magic, and call themselves witches.

Children need to understand that these things are evil and are not to be meddled in. With the flood of books on magic, witches and ghosts, great care is needed when handling this sort of question. Once again, children need to be reassured that the power of God is stronger than the agents of darkness.

Of course, a flat 'No, don't read that book' is fatal. It immediately arouses curiosity! But a gentle, firm warning against this literature and against meddling with anything to do with the occult is necessary.

Questions about witches often come up at Halloween. Until quite recently Halloween parties with games such as 'bobbing apples on water', pumpkin lanterns and dressing up as witches were thought of as fun and just part of a child's social calendar – like bonfire night on 5 November. But nowadays opinion is changing. With the upsurge in occult practices, and a greater fascination with white and black magic, Halloween is seen by many as potentially dangerous, because it is on the fringe of the occult and could lead to a deeper involvement. This is why many Christian parents do not allow their children to go to Halloween parties.

Problems also arise with school celebrations. One mother, a member of her local school Parent-Teacher Association, not wishing to be a kill-joy but firmly believing that Christians should not celebrate Halloween, suggested that the school have an All Saints' Day party with the dressing-up theme taken from *The Narnia Chronicles*.

Why do they say witches appear at Halloween?

Halloween has been celebrated for centuries. It began as a pagan festival, when it was a witches' celebration. The church changed it to a celebration on the eve of All Saints' Day (All Hallows' Even), 1 November. That's why witches are associated with Halloween.

Is it true that witches come out at Halloween and turn you into animals?

No!

Occasionally, it might be as well to find out why a child asks this question. With so many fringe occult books around, suspect fringe occult games and the possibility that they have heard something about it on television, it may be they are very frightened. It is not advisable to go into detail about the occult with young children, except where they may have become involved for some reason. Some children need a lot of reassurance that nothing can hurt them. God is greater than any evil power and his help is always available – not just to children in need, but adults too.

What's magic?

(a nine-year-old)
There are some really clever people who are very skilled at what they call 'magic'. You've seen them on television sometimes . . . when they make it look as if people have disappeared, or make rabbits come out of hats. They can do

Is heaven where the sea and sky meet?

amazing tricks. We can't see how they do them, so we sometimes say, 'It's magic.' But it isn't really.

It's always advisable to err on the side of caution when answering questions on these subjects, as children can so easily be frightened. And it's wise to keep off them at night!

Are there such things as ghosts?

One mother reassured her frightened five-year-old daughter by replying 'No. Nothing in a white sheet will come and get you in the night.' To her eleven-year-old son, on a different occasion, she answered: 'It seems that there may be something. It isn't a person coming back. But perhaps a strong "presence" sometimes remains – just as houses can have a happy or sad feel. If so, they must be spirits. Some people may imagine they have seen a ghost or be misled by poor light, or their own fears.'

*   *   *

Will the world end?

(worried eight-year-old)
Yes, some day, but maybe not for thousands of years yet. There is no need for you to worry. If people are silly enough to start a nuclear war, that will end life as we know it, but it doesn't necessarily mean a total end to the world. Before it finally ends the Bible says that Jesus will come back for the people who love him. And the Bible says that there will be a new heaven and a new earth when this world ends.

Why doesn't God come down now?

God has decided the time when Jesus will return to earth, but nobody except God himself knows when that will be. God is very patient and he is giving people the chance to stop being selfish and careless and disobedient, and to decide to follow Jesus. Christians are told to pray, and to be ready for Jesus' return at any time.

4

Questions about the world

I wonder why the grass is green,
And why the wind is never seen?

Who taught the birds to build a nest,
And told the trees to take a rest?

O, when the moon is not quite round,
Where can the missing bit be found?

Who lights the stars, when they blow out,
And makes the lightning flash about?

Who paints the rainbow in the sky,
And hangs the fluffy clouds so high?

Why is it now, do you suppose,
That Dad won't tell me, if he knows?

'I wonder' from *Come Follow Me*, by Jeannie Kirby

What if the world stops – will we fall off?

Why does life begin at forty, Daddy?

How does God know how many hairs you've got on your head?

When he made us he put them in and counted them.

Where does your lap go when you stand up?

Why do people spend too much money, eat too much, drink too much, argue with the family and then say they've had a lovely Christmas?

Joan's parents are very rich.

How do you know?

Because her parents have a bed each, not like my Mummy and Daddy who have only one.

You know, smacking doesn't make me any gooder, Daddy.

Can thunder pop balloons?

Daddy, what do whales eat for tea?

Who is in charge of the whole world?

Where is the deep end in the sea?

How do we catch electricity?

Why can't they convert empty shops and buildings into homes for people?

Is there any other race but the human race?

Part of a child's attraction is his delight, and sometimes total absorption, in the 'simple things of life', things which may seem small and insignificant to adults.

It is not the aim of this book to deal with all the questions children ask about their world. This selection is simply an attempt to portray the fascinating way in which a child looks at and wonders about the world.

How did an oak tree fit inside an acorn?
(four-year-old)
It didn't! An acorn is a seed. Inside it is everything that is needed for it to grow into an oak tree if it gets enough water, air and sunlight. (This is best illustrated by growing an acorn in water in a glass jar, or by showing the child a tiny shoot if it's the right time of year. Point out trees at different stages of growth, and compare them with the way people grow.)

Why doesn't the sky fall?
(five-year-old)
Because it doesn't exist! It isn't solid or heavy enough to fall. What we see as the sky is just light and dust. They form a thick layer all around the earth which we call 'sky'.

How did the spaceman stay on the moon?
By a force called gravitational attraction. Large objects attract other objects towards their centres. It's the same 'pull' which keeps us on the earth's surface. Without it we would float away. The moon is large enough to attract and hold a person on its surface.

Why doesn't the world stop?
(seven-year-old)
Our world is part of a system of planets which travel around the sun. This movement continues because there is no force to make it stop.

*How did God paint the sky blue? He must
have had a long ladder.*

What if the world stopped? Would we fall off?
(eight-year-old)

No. Gravitational attraction would still pull us towards the centre of the earth. We would be able to feel the difference if the world was slowing down, in the same way that we can feel a car or train braking. But if it had stopped spinning, we would feel just the same as we do now.

How long will the world last?

We don't know. We could change it by a nuclear war so that it would be unrecognizable. In hundreds of millions of years' time, it could be burnt up by the sun. But the Bible tells us that God has decided how long the world will last and that we are not meant to know when it will end.

How did God make bright colours?
(nine-year-old)

God made light, and white light is a mixture of all the colours. When we look at a rainbow, drops of water are splitting the light up, so that we can see the colours separately. We can see the colours because God gave us eyes which are able to detect how much red, how much green and how much blue there is in whatever we look at. The sensitive cells in our eyes send messages to our brains. We say a rose is red because it has red-coloured pigments in its petals. When white light shines on it, the rose absorbs all the colours except the red. It reflects red and so our eyes see the colour red.

How did God make the water we drink?
(nine-year-old)

We know what water is made of: hydrogen and oxygen. But we shall probably never know exactly *how* God made out of nothing all the substances which make up our world.

Did God make cars?

No. He didn't make them himself. When God made the world,

he put people in charge. He gave us raw materials, like the minerals in the earth. And God made us able to work things out and make use of all that he's provided for us on earth. Over the years, people have invented more and more objects and machines. Cars were invented less than 100 years ago.

How did God make us? It must have been horrid putting our insides together!
(eight-year-old)

Our physical bodies are just a very complicated way of putting the same ingredients together – mainly as carbon, hydrogen, oxygen and nitrogen. Our insides are beautiful because they are perfect for doing the job they were meant to do.

When will I be big?
(four-year-old)

It takes a long time to grow up into a grown-up person, years and years. Once you were a tiny baby who couldn't walk or talk (show a photo). You are much bigger than that now, aren't you? So you are getting bigger already. It's rather nice being little though, so you enjoy it. When you get big like me, you'll think how fast the time has gone.

Why do I have to go to school?
(four-year-old)

To be with your friends, and to learn to read and write and to do sums; and to do all your lessons and have play-times with the teachers, so that one day you will be able to go out to work and make a new home and family of your own.

What makes my blood go round inside me?
(five-year-old)

Your heart. (Show them where it is and let them feel it beating.) It's like a pump, sending your blood to all parts of your body and then back again. It never stops – not even when you're in bed and asleep.

What keeps my hair growing?
(four-year-old)
God gave us hair on our heads to protect it – rather like a
crash-helmet and a sun-hat. But when the hair gets too long it
starts to split, so new hair keeps growing to keep your head
covered up.

*   *   *

Encounters with children whose skin is a different colour
often leads to questions, especially in areas which are not as
racially mixed as most inner cities. Some of the questions
which follow are sad. Some reflect the way children absorb
adult prejudices. Some, as in the handicap section, simply
reveal misunderstanding – and the gap between what children make of what they see, and what adults do.

The question, 'How can he be an English champion if he's
a Pakistani?' is easily answered. Being English – or any other
nationality – is not a matter of skin colour, but of citizenship
and where we are born.

So too is the question of a three-year-old who refused to
sit next to an Indian boy. 'Why do I have to sit next to him
when he never washes his hands?' As her mother was quick to
explain, 'It's not that he doesn't wash his hands. He does. But
his skin is brown, not white, and it's meant to be that colour.'

We have to do all we can to prevent childish misunderstanding developing into prejudice and cruelty. A five-year-
old Anglo-Jamaican boy was provoked into saying: 'Why do
they say brown is yuk? They are lying. It's pink babies that are
yuk.'

Why are people black and white?
People's skins are different colours in different parts of the
world. God made us so that we are suited to different climates.
But now that people can travel so easily, black and brown and
white people often live near to one another. We all take after
our parents, so the colour of our skin and hair and eyes

depends on what they look like, not on where we are born.
Although we may look different, God loves and cares for every
one of us. We are all important to him.

Why can't I be brown, not deep black?
Why can't I be white?
(eight-year-old)
Children take after their parents. You are black because Daddy
and I are both black. In the hotter parts of the world most
people are black. God gave them a dark skin so that the hot
sun would not burn them.

Why is she black, but her mummy is white?
(five-year-old)
Her daddy's family comes from a country where the people
are black and her mummy's family come from a country where
the people are white. She has inherited her daddy's skin
colour.

If I stay in the sun will I go as brown as Nicholas?
(a five-year-old with a friend whose family came from Africa)
No, you wouldn't go as brown as Nicholas but you might go
very red and burn. Nicholas is brown because his parents have
a brown skin. They come from a part of the world where
everyone's skin is brown.

Why aren't white/black people friends with us?
Many, many black and white people *are* friends. But there are
many reasons why black people and white people sometimes
find it difficult to be friends. It's always sad when people with
different colour skins can't be friends. Sometimes it's because
people are afraid of others who are different. It can be because
we do not understand each other's culture – the way we live.
And sometimes it's because humans are greedy and want to
keep things for themselves. Don't forget, people with the
same colour skins are not always friends!

Despite these questions, from talking to a number of teachers it would appear that children normally accept a different colour of skin – yellow, brown, black or white – just as they would different colour hair or eyes. It's when they hear adults or older children making racist comments that they begin to notice in a new and wrong way. Though fear too may influence their reactions, as can also happen when children are handicapped in some way.

A six-year-old who had been brought up in a predominantly white area and whose parents bent over backwards to accept anyone of any colour into their home showed great reluctance to communicate with or even to meet black students. The reason was found through a question: 'Will I turn black if I touch them?' Reassured about this, all was well.

Another white five-year-old boy proudly told his mother that he had made friends with a coloured boy at school. When she asked the friend's name her son replied, 'I don't know.'

'What did you say to him?'

'I didn't say anything.'

'But how did you make friends, if you didn't speak?'

'Oh, I just reached out and touched his hair. It was lovely.'

Why do different coloured people punish each other – haven't they got any manners?

We have a long way to go in accepting each other as we are. Sometimes it's fear, sometimes greed, sometimes because we are so different in attitude and upbringing, and in religion too, that we fail to understand one another.

This question came from a seven-year-old, and most of the questions about why people are different colours were asked by seven- and eight-year-olds. When it came to the under-sevens, they were more interested in, 'Why do we wear skin?'

*　　　*　　　*

The questions children ask about the world around them are

not restricted to observation of the natural world. The latest invasion, talk of a third world war and, even more frightening, discussion concerning a possible nuclear war, does not pass over children's heads unnoticed. They are quite likely to ask questions such as 'Is there going to be another war?' or 'Will the next war be a bomb that will make people die?'

Some parents feel that young children need to be protected from too much exposure to what is going on in the world. With sensitive children who are easily frightened, it may be wise tactfully to censor television programmes, especially news bulletins.

Others believe that facts should be faced and that it is wrong to pretend it can't happen. One such mother explained to her (slightly older) children:

'We pray to God that there won't be another war. But there are many dangerous situations in the world which could lead to war. We are all using up the world's coal and oil. Whoever controls the energy resources could bring the rest of the world under their control. There are people so greedy for wealth and power and land that they will stop at nothing. A world war could have broken out many times since the Second World War, but fortunately there is great reluctance to start a war because of the terrible consequences.'

She also quoted examples of God's provision for his people and special help in times of need, even against great odds: Noah and Moses in the Bible and, in the twentieth century, people like the missionary Gladys Aylward ('the small woman') or Dutch Christian Corrie ten Boom in the death-camps of Europe.

On the positive side, there is also a need to teach children to pray for leaders and governments. One mother asked her ten-year-old who he prayed for each night. He answered, 'The President of America and peace in the world.'

Is it right to go to war?
If I was on an aircraft carrier and there was a war and

we were ordered to sink it with a big crew, would it be right to want to win?

(an eight-year-old with an ambition to join the navy)
Some people, called pacifists, believe that it is never right to go to war. Obviously it's always wrong to start a war. But the reason we have armies and navies is to protect us. If another nation attacks us, meaning to do a great deal of wrong, it may be better even to go to war than to let them do what they want. That is why we fought the Second World War.

If we go to war to stop something evil, we want to win. That may mean we have to sink the enemy ship, knowing that some of the crew will die. We don't want them to die. We do all we can to save their lives. But to let the ship through may mean a longer war, and even more lives lost. It's a terrible decision to have to make.

What is God doing when the battleships go down?

(a seven-year-old, after watching an old war film)
Feeling very sad, I should think. God must grieve over the dreadful things we do in wartime. He doesn't put a stop to those things, because when he made us he wanted us to be free to choose – not like robots who can only do as he says. He wants us to choose to love him and be like him. If we all did that, there'd be no more wars.

British and American war films still perpetuate the image of the Germans as 'the enemy', and children soon pick this up. One mother, sitting on a beach not far from a German family one summer holiday, was acutely embarrassed to hear her offspring shout to one another as they tore up a nearby sand-dune: 'Here's your gun (a lolly stick). You be the Germans and I'll shoot you dead!'

Is there going to be a nuclear war?

Everybody in the world hopes not. Many world leaders are doing all they can to ban nuclear weapons. I believe God is in control of his world and will not allow it to be totally destroyed. What's important is for you to remember that God loves you and will take care of you always. Many, many people are doing all in their power to prevent nuclear war.

Deirdre Rhys-Thomas was asked this question by her son, Theo. She was so disturbed that she was unable to answer it that she wrote to world leaders, national figures, entertainers asking them how they would answer the question. A book has been published containing their answers. Asked on a radio programme if this had helped alleviate his 'nuclear nightmare', Theo replied that it had, because it had given him hope. The worst of his fear was not knowing anything about it. Seeing his Mum actually sitting down and writing these letters had made him feel that there was something that could be done and gave him more confidence and faith in the ability of himself and others to do something about preventing it.

Why do we fight?

Why do *you* fight? If you watch two small children playing together and they both want the same toy, what happens? We are all selfish. We fight because we are denied something we want, or we may fight to defend someone. Countries fight over land usually, or for the wealth the land possesses – because people are basically greedy. Sometimes a country will fight to defend another country if it is invaded.

If there is another war, will the whole world be fighting?

Probably not. There are wars being fought at the moment, but not every country is involved.

Younger children are excited by war, war games, tanks, guns and rockets, and also by heroics such as the rescue of hostages. 'That's great! Real James Bond stuff!' was a reaction from her class quoted by one teacher.

Some children may not be bothered about hurt and death, unless a relative or friend dies and then it brings it onto a personal level. The evil in the world is often brought frighteningly near home if a house is burgled, a granny mugged or a child assaulted. Other children may be killed needlessly in bomb attacks, earthquakes or by dying from starvation. They can't understand why the innocent should suffer.

What did they do?
Why are they being punished for something they didn't do?
Why should the children suffer?
(six-year-old)
Why do they have to go without food?
(seven-year-old)
It's grown-up people doing it – they should know better. They are supposed to teach us. How can we honour them?
(nine-year-old)
It wasn't anything they did. They are no worse than the rest of us. Things are unfair in the world because it is no longer as God intended it to be. He is good and just, but people don't want to be like him, they'd rather please themselves.

It's because many of us are greedy, selfish and thoughtless that some people in the world are hungry. We take all we want of the earth's resources. We don't share. So some have too much while others have too little.

Why doesn't God stop hurricanes and floods and earthquakes?
In some parts of the world, there is a greater risk of these disasters happening than in others because the earth is more unstable, because forests have been chopped down, or because of the type of weather. Sometimes homes are built in dangerous areas because people don't understand the risks

or have nowhere else to live. So, when disaster strikes, they are killed.

This, of course, is only part of the answer. What this and many other related questions are really asking is 'Why suffering?' It must be one of the oldest questions in the world. It is certainly one of the hardest to answer. We have suggested some possibilities already in the section on death.

From the Bible it is clear that pain was not part of God's original intention for us. Suffering is caused by the presence of evil in the world. It is not a direct punishment for the wrongdoing of an individual.

God sets limits to pain and suffering. He helps and comforts us in it. He teaches us and others through it. He himself has shared it, in the person of Jesus. And the suffering of Jesus has won us pardon and freedom.

Death itself need no longer be the end. It is not the worst thing that can happen to us, and not the end of everything. It is the beginning of something far better than anything we have yet known.

Why does God let people do wicked things?

When God created men and women, he gave them the freedom to choose how to behave. He did not make them like robots. In the Bible we can read God's laws, where he sets out how we should live. And God sent Jesus to show us how to live. If people choose not to obey God's laws, then bad things happen and people do wicked things.

Why do people steal and kill?

Sometimes people who steal and kill can't help it. Their minds are sick. They need our help. Others are greedy, envious or cruel and give in to the evil inside them. If people disobey God's commands, they have no rules other than their own selfishness to live by. So, if they want something, they take it, and if they hate someone they may kill them.

WILL MY RABBIT GO TO HEAVEN?

How can we look after other people? Does that mean they have to come and live with us?

No, not usually. There are lots of ways that we can show that we care for those around us and that we want to make them happy. We can share our games and toys with other children, do errands for Gran and Grandad or give some of our pocket money to a charity. Mum often needs help at home or somebody may need help with their shopping. There are lots of opportunities for 'looking after' other people if we keep our eyes and ears open.

Why can't I swear?

A lot of swear-words are ways of misusing the name of God. If we love God we won't want to use his name like that, or to upset other people by swearing. (At some time or other children come home from school with four-letter sex words, and try them out. If the meaning of these words, and other people's sensitivities are explained, most children respect this, provided the words are not bandied about at home!)

Why can't I do what I like?

(six-year-old)

Because whatever we do or say affects other people. What you want to do at a particular time may hurt or upset somebody else. God created us to be with other people, so you must think what they would like too.

*   *   *

Why do we have conservation?

So that we can pass on all the lovely and beautiful things in the world to your children and your children's children. Sadly, people in the industrialized world have been greedy in using an unfair share of the world's resources. We have also polluted the land, air and water with rubbish which will not break down and chemicals which destroy living plants and creatures – and the forests. We have to stop before it is too late.

Much is being done in schools and in the media to make children far more aware of conservation than in previous generations.

A primary school teacher with twenty-five years' experience noted the changing attitudes in one simple situation. Outside her classroom window an enormous bulldozer was clearing up after tree-felling. Her latest group of five-year-olds dashed to the window and remarked, 'Oh, look Miss, they've cut down our trees!' Not so long before, it would have been, 'Oh, look Miss, there's a huge bulldozer!'

A five-year-old at home was watching her parents dig up a privet hedge one day when she sasked, 'Do you think God will mind you doing that?'

Why do we have trees?
Why do we need to look after them?

If trees and plants are not taken care of they die, like any other living thing.

Our world needs trees and plants for all sorts of reasons . . . oxygen, food, shelter, wood, etc. They help to stop the soil being blown or rained away. They also provide us with much beauty. Many of the world's trees are being cut down and we need to do all we can to protect them.

Why do people kill animals?

For various reasons. To begin with people killed animals in order to survive – for food, for clothes and for protection. The Eskimos used every bit of the animals they killed, and they needed to kill in order to live. Now we over-kill. Often this is unnecessary as other commodities can be used. It is sheer greed. Unlike the Eskimos, we do not need furs to keep warm. Sometimes animals are killed for research. Much is being done to prevent the large animals like elephants and tigers being killed. Otters and badgers are being looked after too, and other species which are in danger of dying out altogether if we continue to kill them. Whales are a good example. We no longer need their meat or their oil.

How did conservation get started?

In the beginning, when God made people to live in his world he put them in charge of everything and told them to take care of it all. But we grew greedy, using up more and more, and spoiling the world. Now we have to struggle to keep it useful and beautiful, and to prevent real disaster. Well-known people like David Bellamy, members of the Green Party, as well as many other individuals and organizations, are doing all they can to preserve and keep the world a good place in which to live and to hand on to the next generations. Every one of us can help, even if it is only in a small way.

Why should we pick up other people's rubbish?

If we take care of the world around us, life is better for everyone. Some people don't think that matters. But if we want to look after God's world, we will be upset if people drop litter or break bottles in the road or write on walls. If we show that we care about our surroundings, perhaps other people will notice and follow our example.

*   *   *

Is there a Father Christmas?

Well, is there? You certainly see a lot around in December. Assuming that it's always wrong to lie, you could throw the question back. Ask your child, 'What do you think?' and hedge!

A child usually asks this question when a friend has told him that there isn't a Father Christmas. If he wants to go on believing, he'll happily kid himself and so can you! Father Christmas always comes to our house and always will, even though nobody says they believe in him and nobody says they don't! But I did tell my daughter that if she doesn't

I'm not writing this to offend you, God, but why haven't I had a white Christmas yet?

believe in him any more, she's not to spoil anyone else's fun by deliberately saying he doesn't exist.

However, to feed children's imaginations too much about Father Christmas is not a good idea. They sometimes end up confusing him with God, possibly because they can't see him, he's old and good and has a beard! Some children are genuinely frightened at the thought of a man coming down the chimney and need to be reassured along the lines of 'No, Father Christmas won't come down the chimney. Daddy will bring the toys up for you', or 'Daddy (or Mummy) will be here – don't worry. Go to sleep now, or no toys!' Once, in our house, Father Christmas got the stockings muddled, and there were shrieks of agony at 5 a.m. when our ten-year-old son opened one containing dollies' clothes!

5

Questions about sex and family life

'I suppose I shall have to be married some day,' said Peter. 'But it will be an awful bother having her around all the time. I'd like to marry a lady who had trances and only woke up once or twice a year.'

From *The Railway Children*, by E. Nesbit

Where did I come from?

'Why didn't God send clothes with the new baby? She needs them.'
Older brother: 'Don't be stupid. God can't knit!'

Does the baby have first course through one boob and pudding through the other?

Aids, Aids, Aids ... that's all we hear about all day long. There's only one programme it's not been on and that's 'Playschool'.

A young girl told her school friends:

My Mum takes Aids tablets.

Will she go to hospital? Will she die?

No. They're slimming tablets.

Mummy, why did you have two children – because you've only got two boobs to feed us with?

A cross five-year-old to the nurse:
'Why is this new baby eating my Mum? She's a menace. As you brought her here, why can't you take her back?'

Is your guineapig a boy or a girl?

It's a he ... and a she at weekends.

Miss, how do you spell sex?

That's an interesting word. Why do you want to know?

Well, I'm writing about in-sects. I can do the in bit, but I can't cope with the sex.

'Did you mix me up like that cake, Mummy?' asked a four-year-old, as he peered into the mixing bowl.

That brings us to one section of questions which a book on children's questions cannot possibly omit!

Whereas a child marvels at the fascinating and ingenious way he has been made, an adult can be acutely embarrassed at having to give the required information – and usually it is only a point of information that is wanted. But however well-informed grown-ups pride themselves on being on sex education, the questions can knock them for six.

Just as the 'Where does God live?' question comes up at the most inconvenient time, so the 'Where did I come from?' poser arises at the most embarrassing moment. It can arrive at any time, in any form and at an early age, from our curious and intrigued offspring – or, even worse, from someone else's curious, intrigued offspring!

During the school-run with a car-load of neighbours' children of varying ages, a five-year-old piped up with, 'Mummy, how do babies come?' His seven-year-old brother replied on behalf of his mother, as she negotiated a difficult bend: 'Don't be silly, Edward. You know that the A.I. man comes.' (A.I. is 'artificial insemination', or the impregnation of the female by artificial means.) This particular family lived on a farm! It is perhaps easier to explain 'the facts of life' to country children as they are happening all around them, quite naturally – but mistakes can happen.

Learning to be open and honest with children when it comes to sex education is not as easy as we, in this so-called permissive age, like to think. The Victorian attitude to sex is taking much longer to die than many of us realize. We are still greatly influenced by our own parents' attitudes and, as individuals, we have differing views and opinions on how best to explain this healthy and natural part of life.

The book of Proverbs in the Bible says, 'Train up a child in the way he should go'. Just as in any other area of life, parents are responsible for instructing their children in sexual matters, and this responsibility should not be abdicated. How much more appropriate that a child should learn about this area of life naturally, within the family, than that he should glean his information in whispers behind the bike-shed at school or from the scribbles on lavatory walls.

Being able to answer young children's questions about sexual matters – some of which are phrased in the most amusing ways – can make communication so much easier during those turbulent adolescent years. It's likely, too, that most questions in this sphere will be asked of us before the child is eleven or twelve.

There are many books available in libraries and book-shops to help parents understand, explain and answer their children's questions. We do not have to know all the answers ourselves. Obtaining information from a book helps to make this a joint exercise, and a shared experience. Children are used to visual instruction and many of these books have simple, clear illustrations. Communicating by words can leave large gaps in our explanations. Telling a four- or five-year-old with a vivid imagination that the baby is in 'Mummy's tummy' can cause him concern when he sees Mummy munching her toast and marmalade at breakfast!

Of course, there is one snag about books. You aren't usually carrying them around when the how, when, why question comes up on the bus! One mother, sitting at the front of a bus while her five-year-old stared out of the window from the back seat, was jerked out of her serenity with the shout: 'Hey, Mum! Does the chicken's egg drop out of its bottom like I dropped out of you?'

'Where did my baby sister come from?' a four-year-old asked the vicar outside church one morning, as she pulled back the pram blanket to show him.

'She grew inside Mummy's tummy,' was the calm reply.

Some children will remain satisfied with that answer while others, fascinated, may continue like this three-year-old:

Did you eat Ben, Mummy?

No, I didn't eat him. When a daddy and a mummy want a baby, the daddy puts his sperm into the mummy's tummy where it will join with an egg and gradually grow into a baby.

How did I get out?

You came out of a hole between my legs.

Questions like these come up at different ages and often several times. How much information to give sometimes bothers parents. As long as we answer the actual question, that's usually enough. If the time is very awkward – and just occasionally a child will ask you such a question to see your reaction – then explain that you will answer it later and perhaps look at a book together. But make sure it's done that same day.

The trickiest question of the lot (to you, not the child), perhaps because it is so personal, comes up sooner or later. Let's hope it's sooner – it's easier to explain to a five-year-old than to a ten-year-old.

How did Daddy put his sperm into your tummy?

Daddy puts his penis inside Mummy's vagina, which is an opening between her legs. The sperm which has been made in his testicles (two little bags between his legs) travels from his penis up Mummy's vagina and into her womb. That is a place in the lower part of her tummy where the baby will grow.

Having explained all this to her six-year-old daughter, coolly and clinically, or so she thought, one mother was somewhat taken aback when her little girl looked up and said, 'But Mummy, how can Daddy do it with his pyjamas on?'

A sensitive eight-year-old, worried by such an explanation, immediately asked:

Does it hurt, Mummy?

No, when a mummy and daddy love each other very much, they want to come close together, cuddle and make love. Sometimes they want to make a baby together. It is a loving act between a husband and a wife.

How long did I take to grow?

(seven-year-old)

Nine months. The sperm from Daddy together with the egg produced in Mummy's ovaries grew over a period of nine months into a baby inside Mummy's 'uterus' or womb. That's the special place inside a mother's tummy where the baby grows until he or she is ready to be born.

What did I eat in your tummy?

(six-year-old)

You shared my food. A baby is attached to the mummy's tummy by a tube and it is through this that food in liquid form passes into the baby.

Will I get married when I grow up?

(five-year-old)

Lots of people get married when they grow up. But not everyone does. Some find somebody to love and want to marry them. Some like to be on their own. You won't really know the answer until you grow up as big as Mummy and Daddy.

Why can't I marry Daddy when I grow up?

(doting four-year-old)

When you've grown up you will probably find that you will meet someone very special, who thinks you are very special too. You will both decide whether you want to marry each other or not. Daddy is married already. Besides, daddies don't marry their children, just as brothers don't marry their sisters.

Why is your love for me different from your love for Daddy?

There are lots of kinds of loving. Do you love me in exactly the same way as you love your baby brother, or your friend? It's a special kind of love that makes a grown-up man and woman decide to marry one another. And it's another special kind of love that a mummy has for her children.

How do I know when my tummy is ready to have a baby?

(six-year-old)

You cannot have a baby for a long, long time yet. Changes take place inside your body as you grow up which make it ready to have a baby.

Allowing young children to see parents naked can perhaps avoid the following question, which came up during Sunday tea with a rather Victorian grandmother.

'Mummy, why has David got a finger sticking out of his bottom?' piped a clear, three-year-old voice.

'Because he is a boy, dear, and boys are made differently from girls. It is not a finger, it's something called a penis which he uses to pee through. Have a biscuit, Granny!' (It can be explained later that the penis is also used for making babies with.)

Equally, as children get older, their right to privacy needs to be respected.

What are these bags under my penis?

(fascinated five-year-old, in the bath)

They are called testicles. When you have grown up into a man they will contain lots of sperms – too small to see – which, if joined with a mummy's tiny egg, will make a baby.

How are twins made?

(eleven-year-old)

Identical twins look exactly alike and are of the same sex. They are made when an egg and a sperm which have joined together divide. Each half develops into a baby. A mother has two ovaries where her eggs are stored. Normally only one egg is released each month. Twins who aren't identical are made if two eggs are released and fertilized.

Are you in season, Mummy?

(eight-year-old who had not been allowed to take her dog for a walk because it was in season)

No. There are differences between dogs making puppies and humans making babies. A female dog, or bitch, is 'in season' or 'on heat' only twice a year. That is when she is producing an egg ready to be fertilized by a male dog. That is the only time when a dog can make a puppy, but Mummy produces an egg every month.

Sometimes children come across tampon or sanitary-towel machines in public lavatories and want to know what they are. Depending on the circumstances and the age, it could be an opportunity – again later, and with the help of a book – to explain menstruation to both girls and boys. Girls, of course, must be prepared for the onset of their periods in good time.

A simple explanation can be given, as follows: 'Women produce an egg once a month. Unless the egg is fertilized by a male sperm, the spongy lining of the uterus and the special blood supply prepared to nourish it are not needed. So blood and mucus are discarded every month through the vagina. Pads or tampons are used to catch this fluid.'

How can she have a baby without being married?

(seven-year-old)

It's not being married that does it. Once a girl's body is ready to make a baby, usually between the ages of eleven and fifteen, she is able to have a baby if a man makes love to her.

But a girl needs to be grown-up enough in other ways to look after and understand a baby properly. Babies need a tremendous amount of time and care. Once there is a baby around, you can't think just of yourself any more. It wouldn't be easy to go out and have fun. Getting a job and looking after the baby would be difficult. Besides, daddies like to look after babies too. If you are not grown-up enough to look after yourselves properly, you can't really look after a baby properly.

God created us to be in families. He wants a baby to have a mummy and a daddy living together happily in a home where they can help each other to bring up the baby until he or she is able to look after themselves.

Why isn't Mummy going to have a baby now? What's happened to the baby in her tummy?

The parents explained to their six- and eight-year-olds about a miscarriage. 'The baby died. Sometimes, the seed from which a baby grows doesn't develop properly. It shrivels up and dies.' The father was able to take the children down the garden and show them some beans he'd sown the previous winter that had done just that and therefore had never developed. The children accepted this explanation and now, happily, have another beautiful sister. But beware – children can very easily get the wrong idea from the garden seed parallel – or from an egg, come to that.

*   *   *

While watching television, children hear words such as 'rape', 'homosexual', 'abortion', and sometimes will ask what they mean. Often these are subjects that their parents would not have discussed during their own primary school days.

What is rape?

Rape is when a man forces a woman to have sexual intercourse with him.

(For younger children, rape could be explained as 'a man making a nasty attack on a woman'.)

What is a homosexual?
Someone who is sexually attracted to their own sex rather than to the opposite sex – a man to another man, or a woman to another woman.

What is abortion?
It's when a pregnant woman decides to have the fertilized egg that is growing into a baby removed by a doctor before it has had time to develop properly.

What is a prostitute?
(A six-year-old was overheard answering her five-year-old sister: 'It's an Anglican, like we are, of course.')
It's a woman who has sexual intercourse with lots of men and is paid for it.

What is a brothel?
A house where prostitutes live.

What is a flasher?
A flasher is a man who undoes his trousers and shows you his penis – usually in a park or in the street.

How can mummies and daddies not have a baby if they don't want to have one?
There are a number of ways mummies and daddies can prevent having babies. Some mummies take birth control pills; daddies can use condoms, a rubber sheath or tube that fits over his penis. There are clinics that help mummies and daddies to decide which is the best method to have a baby at the right time or for them to prevent too many babies.

What are those pills you are taking?

They are birth control pills to stop my body releasing eggs and therefore making sure I do not have a baby.

*　　*　　*

Aids, Aids, Aids – that's all you hear about on television these days. The only programme it's not been on yet is 'Playschool'.

(nine-year-old)

Don't be silly. How can you fit a condom on Humpty Dumpty?

(her eleven-year-old brother)

With so much publicity about Aids, particularly on television, children are asking questions – and certainly it is talked about in the playgrounds at school.

What they hear and see can be frightening, and some children will need reassurance. There are also many misunderstandings. Six-year-old Simon cried every time he saw the government's publicity about Aids. His parents could not understand why, until he explained that he had always wanted to be an airline pilot and now he couldn't. Why not? they asked. Because he had picked up a report that pilots were in the high risk group for Aids. If he became a pilot he would die – and he didn't want to die. Similarly, children who had heard the slogan, 'Don't die of ignorance', were worried about catching that!

Although some parents are concerned that questions about Aids introduce children to sex in the wrong way, talking about Aids can in fact be a good opportunity for general health and sex education. Each parent will have some idea of how much their child can understand, and the age of the child will obviously determine how much they tell him/her. The following are simply guide-line answers to some difficult questions.

What is Aids?

(five-year-old)

Aids is a serious disease.

What is Aids?

(nine-year-old)

The initials AIDS stand for Acquired Immune Deficiency Syndrome. Aids is a very serious illness caused by a virus which makes a person unable to fight off other infections. So he or she may die. There is as yet no cure for Aids, which is why there is so much publicity to try to prevent it.

Will I get it?

(five-year-old)

No. You can't catch Aids like a cold or chickenpox.

If more information is needed, you could go on to explain that it is not caught through swimming in a pool, from the air, or from ordinary contact with people. Should the child go on to ask, 'How do you get it, then?', you may want simply to say that you will explain when the child is older, as it is difficult to understand. You could say that it is passed on through body fluids – though this is difficult to explain without creating needless worry in young children. Literature is available at clinics to help parents and children to understand more about Aids.

Will you get it, Mummy?

(five-year-old)

No, because I know how to prevent it.

How do you get Aids?

(nine-year-old)

Aids is spread from person to person mainly through sexual intercourse with someone who has Aids or is a 'carrier' of the condition. Drug addicts are also specially at risk if they inject themselves with needles other people have used. Aids is passed on through body fluids and blood. You can't catch it by shaking hands or from toilet seats, nor by mouth-to-mouth resuscitation. The very best way to prevent Aids spreading is to keep sexual intercourse for marriage and to be faithful to one partner, which is what God intended and planned as the best and happiest way for people to live.

*   *   *

Why do strangers hurt children?
Why do parents have children in the first place if they are only going to abuse them?
Who can I tell?

Just as we teach children road sense, warn about fire and tell them not to play with live wires or power points so we have a duty to protect them against possible child abuse.

For years we have taught them not to talk to strangers. Now we need to check that they are aware of the possibility of abuse from someone they know. How do you begin to talk to children about such a sensitive subject without frightening them, making them ultra-suspicious of adults, or reluctant to receive normal everyday affection?

It is beyond the scope of this book to provide the help that is needed. But *The Willow Street Kids* is a book specially written for children by Michele Elliott, mother of two and an educational psychologist. It is a collection of true stories told by children and aims to make them less vulnerable to danger, encouraging them to think about how to handle different situations that may confront them. The stories include a stranger approaching a child in the street; bullies; a flasher; upsetting telephone calls and being touched by an older person in a way which makes them feel uncomfortable. Reading about the children helping each other, the teacher who taught them how to keep safe, and how the individuals coped with these potentially dangerous situations is reassuring to child and parent. (Other helpful books in this area are Oralie

Wachter's *No More Secrets for Me*, and *Sexual Abuse: Let's talk about it* by Margaret O. Hyde.)

Michele Elliott has also written a practical guide called *Keeping Safe*. It gives information for parents on how to start teaching young children how to keep safe and includes fun learning games to introduce the idea to children, helping them to develop skills to protect themselves, thus making them less vulnerable to danger.

In answer to the question, 'Why do parents have children in the first place, if they are only going to abuse them?', we can say that usually parents want their children very much and do everything they can to love and keep them safe. Sometimes it may happen that a parent seriously hurts a child and then there is something wrong. Stress and inability to cope with difficult situations or a mental illness may cause them to react in an abnormal way. They need help, and that may even mean in extreme cases them going to prison, to stop them hurting children.

Care needs to be taken here that a parent or teacher knows why this question has been asked. Was it prompted by something they saw on television, read about, or heard at school? Or are they trying to say something much more difficult . . . that they have been abused in some way?

Practical help is available in most countries through child protection and family crisis services, and community welfare. In Britain, Kidscape is a campaign providing practical help for all children (with parents, teachers and others) to keep them safe from dangers – particularly from sexual assault. They maintain that only to warn children about strangers is like teaching them 'to cross the road and only watch for red cars'. Parents can help their children by teaching them how to recognize dangerous situations and inappropriate touching; to say 'No' and get away; to refuse to keep 'bad secrets'. Kidscape claims that children who know what to do in potentially dangerous situations are not only less at risk but are also more confident. The campaign's slogan is 'Good Sense

Defence' and teaching kits are provided for schools and parents, with ten golden rules for keeping safe. In Australia and the United States, individual states have agencies which provide help and information.

*   *   *

A child's experience of family life may not always be a happy, relaxed, secure affair. Permissive attitudes to sex and the high incidence of marriage breakdown in our society mean that children may be left with a single parent – or no parents at all. This final section attempts to deal with questions which may arise from these very situations: the adopted child who wants to know where his 'first mum' is or the child of divorced parents who can't understand why daddy left home.

Adoption needs to be talked about as part of everyday life from an early age, and gradually explained in a way appropriate to the child's level of understanding. If the word 'adoption' is used from babyhood, it becomes natural and familiar.

Here is one family's experience:

'Our daughter grew up accepting adoption as a fact of life . . . although we did have some problems when she announced to people she was "doctored". From the time she could first understand, we explained that unfortunately her first mum had been unable to keep her. We explained why, bit by bit, so that she could understand. She had been loved very much and her mum had made every effort to keep her. We laid great stress on this, keeping some of her pretty baby clothes and cuddly toys so that she could see that was true.

'We do have problems when our other children want to hear the story of their birth, but we tell the tale of the day we collected her from the nursery. Fortunately the adoption officer pointed out the need to make that a day of celebration. The older two remember the ride on the train, the day in the park and the knickerbocker glory, although the actual court proceedings were a bit of a non-event. Now she likes to see her special papers (adoption certificate) that prove she is a

'Why do Mummy and Daddy sleep in the same bed?'
Her sister: 'It's instead of a hot-water bottle.'

member of our family.'

Another couple, whose three adopted children arrived with nothing from their original mums, tell how one of them was found by the social services in only a nappy. But 'we still say that his mum wanted what was best for him, knowing that she couldn't look after him herself. We have made a story book of their arrivals and court cases but tend to celebrate birthdays and Christmas rather than the "Coming Days".'

Every family's experiences and explanations will be slightly different; however, in each case we might add that every Christian is an 'adopted' child of God – a member of his family, loved and chosen.

What does 'adoption' mean?
(four-year-old)
If a mummy and daddy want babies but have none of their own, they sometimes adopt a baby or a boy or girl whose own mummy and daddy cannot look after him (or her) properly. Adoption means that they take this child into their home, and love and care for him as if he were their own child. It means that they choose him for their very own and that he belongs to their family.

Why didn't my first mum keep me? Didn't she love me?
She wanted to keep you very much but she could see that there would be lots of problems later on. She didn't have a husband or a proper home. And she would have had to go out to work leaving you with somebody else. She loved you very much – so much that she had to part with you because she couldn't look after you in the way she wanted.

Will I ever see my first mum?
Some new laws have been introduced which mean that one day you will have the right to try to find out where your first mother is. But you will have to think about it very carefully. Your mum might be very different from how you imagine her.

It could create problems for your mum if she has a new family and has never told them about you.

How come you're black, and you've got a white mum?

(asked of a coloured child by friends at school)
Because my real parents were black but they couldn't look after me and I was adopted by a white family and I live in their home now.

Why do my real mummy and daddy look after my baby brother and not me?

(a five-year-old to her foster-mum)
Because your mummy isn't well enough to look after two children at the same time and so we are looking after you until she is better. Babies need an awful lot of looking after. You're a big girl and you're able to help us. But don't forget that your real mummy loves you very much and we do too.

(Obviously, different situations will require different answers. But it's important for the child to know that he/she may go back to their real parents at some future date.)

*   *   *

Separation and divorce lead inevitably to difficult and painful questions. It's usually the mother who has to answer these, since the children remain in her care. Those who have practical experience of this emphasize that children should never be left to think it is their fault that Daddy/Mummy has left. They should never be told lies. The situation should be explained simply and without bias. It is most important not to turn the child against the absent parent (this can be an even greater temptation for the new marriage partner) or to take out the anger and spite on the children if they resemble the missing parent or pine for him/her.

Although the actual suffering may be more acute before the split — when the quarrelling, fighting and upsets are taking place – divorce is still a bereavement experience. There will be no easy answers, and painful emotions will have to be worked through by adults and children.

Why did Daddy get angry? We didn't do anything. Where has Daddy/Mummy gone? Why has Daddy/Mummy gone?

You know how you fall out with your friends. You argue and don't talk to one another for days. That sometimes happens with mummies and daddies, too. Daddy (Mummy) will always be your Daddy, and he still loves you. But Mummy and Daddy don't love each other any more. So instead of having quarrels which make all of us unhappy, Daddy (Mummy) decided not to live at home any more.

Why won't you have Daddy back?

Sometimes two grown-ups make one another so unhappy that they just cannot carry on living together. Daddy and I would not be happy together any more. One day I'll be able to tell you more about it.

Why can't we all live together?

(five-year-old whose mum married again)
It just wouldn't work. Daddy and I would not be happy and our quarrels would make you unhappy. I'm married to Dave (stepfather) now, not to Daddy, so he lives here with us. What's important is that I love you, Dave loves you and Daddy loves you, too.

What is divorce?

(six-year-old)
Sometimes a man and a woman who are married don't want to be with each other any longer and finally decide to live apart. They have their marriage ended by law and that is called divorce. From then on they are no longer known as husband and wife.

Is it nice having two daddies?

(seven-year-old)

Not really; it's confusing. It might be nice when it comes to having two lots of presents, but happiness isn't just having presents, is it? God meant us to live in families with just one daddy and one mummy. That's best, and no-one plans for their children to have two daddies. But sometimes a mummy and a daddy quarrel so much that one of them goes away. Then they may get married again to somebody different.

Why is Jack's daddy living with Mary's mummy?

(eight-year-old)

Jack's daddy and mummy don't love each other any more, so they don't live with each other. Mary's daddy and mummy don't love each other any more and so they have decided not to live together either.

Jack's daddy and Mary's mummy have decided to live together. It must be very confusing for Jack and Mary. It is very sad, too. When a man and a woman get married in church, they promise to stay together until they are parted by death. That is God's best for people and he is sad when families split up.

Will I see my real mother again?

(an eleven-year-old to her stepmother)

Yes, perhaps one day you will. She is living in Canada now, but I am sure as the years pass she will think about you a lot and wonder what you are like now you're growing up.

Roger's got a daddy, David's got a daddy – why haven't I got a daddy?

(four-year-old)

You have got a daddy but he doesn't live with us any more. But we do have Grandad and Uncle Ben. They're very special and can do lots of things that daddies do.

Do we have to go to Daddy's?
Why didn't Daddy die, then we wouldn't have to keep going backwards and forwards?

Daddy still loves you and wants to see you. Even though he doesn't live with us all the time any more, he wants you to visit him and he enjoys being with you.

In some ways the children asking all these questions were lucky. They had enough confidence in adults, in spite of their painful experiences, still to ask questions. They have less of a problem than those who don't say much, who go to enormous pains to conceal the fact that there is only one parent, and who burst into tears or temper – to the mystification of teachers or other adults who haven't been told of the situation at home.

Mum, isn't God clever – I can't wait to ask him all I wanted to know!

Postscript

There is no end to the questions children ask. The ones we've collected in this book are just the tip of the iceberg. And the questions children ask us often lead to questions of our own. Unless *we* understand, how can we satisfy their eager young minds?

But when it comes to some of their questions, we may feel like this nine-year-old:

'You know all the stories we hear in church,' he said to his mum one day, '... things like the five loaves and the two fishes ... sometimes I find it hard to believe. How could God do things like that? I need to see it to believe it.'

Thomas, one of the twelve close friends of Jesus, felt just like that. He simply would not believe that Jesus had risen from the dead, unless he could see and touch the scars of the crucifixion on Jesus' body.

Jesus said to him, 'Do you believe because you see me? How happy are those who believe without seeing me!'

We all have doubts and questions. We make mistakes and are disappointed with ourselves at times. The important thing is what we do with our mistakes and questions and doubts. Do we go on asking, learning and growing? Or do we give up and not bother to enquire further?

'Ask, and you will receive;' says Jesus, 'seek, and you will find; knock, and the door will be opened to you.' That's a promise for each one of us.

Suggested further reading

There is a whole host of books which could be recommended to help you answer children's questions, but here is just a small selection:

For adults
About Christianity:
> Finding Faith, by Andrew Knowles, Lion Publishing/Lion Publishing Corporation
> You must be joking, by Michael Green, Hodder and Stoughton/ Tyndale House Publishers
> Basic Christianity, by John Stott, Inter-Varsity Press/ Eerdmans
> Know what you believe, by Paul Little, Scripture Union/Victor Books

About death and suffering:
> Joni, by Joni Eareckson, Pickering and Inglis/Zondervan
> A step further, by Joni Eareckson and Steve Estes, Pickering and Inglis/Zondervan
> No easy answers, by Eugenia Price, STL Books/Zondervan (No pat answers)
> The last enemy, by Howard Guinness, Falcon booklet
> A death in the family, by Jean Richardson, Lion Publishing; see the chapter on 'The bereaved child'.

Children at risk:
> Children Under Stress, by Sulu Wolff, Penguin Books
> Keeping Safe, by Michele Elliott, Bedford Square Press

In the UK, the Marriage Guidance Council produces a general list of recommended books and booklets, and also provides a reliable service for those wanting material on marriage and the family, sex education, divorce, adoption, etc. Contact them at the Marriage Guidance Council's Book Department, Little Church Street, Rugby, Warwickshire.

For children

About sex:

Our New Baby, by Marlee and Benny Alex, Lion Publishing

Where did I come from? by Peter Mayle, Macmillan/Lyle Stuart

How You Are Made, by Christina Palmgren, J. M. Dent

For the over nines: Sex and That, by Michael Lawson and Dr David Skipp, Lion Publishing

Love and Sex in Plain Language, by Eric Johnson, Andre Deutsch/Harper & Row

You're nearly there, by Mary Kehle, Pickering and Inglis/Harold Shaw Publishers

About death:

Why did God let Grandpa die? by Phoebe Cranor, Bethany Fellowship, includes some helpful answers.

Grandpa and Me, by Marlee and Benny Alex, Lion Publishing.

Children at risk:

The Willow Street Kids, by Michele Elliott, Pan Piccolo.

No More Secrets for Me, by Oralie Wachter, Penguin Books.

Sexual Abuse: Let's talk about it, by Margaret O. Hyde, Westminster Press.

The Lion Care series for seven- to eleven-year-olds has helpful titles on divorce (Mike's Lonely Summer) and adoption (Andy's Big Question/Mario's Big Question (US)) with more titles planned, by Carolyn Nystrom, Lion Publishing/Lion Publishing Corporation.

SEX AND THAT

What's it all about?

Michael Lawson and Dr David Skipp

'What's happening to me?'
'Am I really normal?'
'Will anyone like me enough to want to go out with me?'
'How far can I go?'
'Mum and Dad don't understand.'

This book answers some of the questions you haven't dared ask – and some you may not have thought of yet. It explains what is happening as you are growing up. It gives practical help in starting new relationships – and keeping them going.

Growing up is about being you. This book helps you learn to live with your feelings and to discover who you really are.

ISBN 0 85648 782 1

CHARNWOOD

Grace Wyatt with Clive Langmead

Charnwood is the name of a very remarkable nursery centre which gives handicapped and normal children the opportunity to play, learn and grow together. Today the experts readily acknowledge the all-round benefits of this kind of integrated learning. In the 1960s, when Grace Wyatt's pioneer work began, it was a very different matter and there were many battles to fight.

This is a story of handicapped children and their families, the agonies and the triumphs. It carries a strong message of hope for all who are in any way involved with handicap, and for the 'normal' too. There is joy in loving a child purely for who he is, and great reward in seeing children with very different abilities play together in a child-world untouched by labels and restrictions.

ISBN 0 7459 1137 4

A selection of top titles from LION PUBLISHING

FAMILY/PRACTICAL HELP

WHO'D BE A MUM! Hanna Ahrens	£1.50	☐
COPING WITH DEPRESSION Myra Chave-Jones	£1.50	☐
SINGLE PARENT Maggie Durran	£1.95	☐
THE LONG ROAD HOME Wendy Green	£1.95	☐
WHEN SOMEONE YOU LOVE IS		
DYING Ruth Kopp	£4.95	☐
SEX AND THAT Michael Lawson/Dr David Skipp	£1.75	☐
SIMPLE SIMON Ann Lovell	£1.50	☐
ELIZABETH JOY Caroline Philps	£1.50	☐
YOUR MARRIAGE Peg and Lee Rankin	£2.50	☐
HOW CAN IT BE ALL RIGHT WHEN		
EVERYTHING IS ALL WRONG? Lewis Smedes	£1.75	☐
MERE MORALITY Lewis Smedes	£1.95	☐
SEX IN THE REAL WORLD Lewis Smedes	£1.95	☐
CHARNWOOD Grace Wyatt/Clive Langmead	£2.50	☐
PICTURES ON THE PAGE Pat Wynnejones	£1.95	☐

All Lion paperbacks are available from your local bookshop or newsagent, or can be ordered direct from the address below. Just tick the titles you want and fill in the form.

Name (Block letters) ....

Address ....

....

Write to Lion Publishing, Cash Sales Department, PO Box 11, Falmouth, Cornwall TR10 9EN, England.

Please enclose a cheque or postal order to the value of the cover price plus:

UK: 55p for the first book, 22p for the second book and 14p for each additional book ordered to a maximum charge of £1.75.

OVERSEAS: £1.00 for the first book plus 25p per copy for each additional book.

BFPO: 55p for the first book, 22p for the second book plus 14p per copy for the next seven books, thereafter 8p per book.

Lion Publishing reserves the right to show on covers and charge new retail prices which may differ from those previously advertised in the text or elsewhere, and to increase postal rates in accordance with the Post Office.